# student WORKB
## AS Chemistry Multiple Choice

GW01549675

# Introduction

This book of multiple-choice and short-answer questions is intended as a revision aid. Having covered a topic area, you can quickly check your understanding by completing the relevant test.

The key areas of AS chemistry are:

- Atoms, moles and the periodic table
- Organic chemistry
- Physical chemistry

For each area there are tests on the key topics, followed by a general test, which covers the whole area. Each multiple-choice question is followed by a short-answer question, resulting in 18 multiple-choice questions and 18 short-answer questions in each test.

It should take you 50 minutes to complete a test. The multiple-choice questions are worth 1 mark each, while the short-answer questions are worth 2 marks. On the next page is a grid on which you can chart your progress.

# Progress check

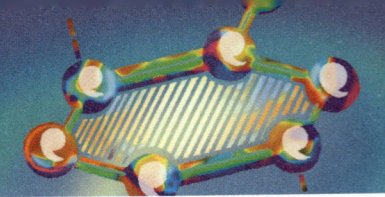

| Topic area | Multiple choice | | Short answers | |
|---|---|---|---|---|
| | Possible score | Your score | Possible score | Your score |
| **Atoms, moles and the periodic table** | | | | |
| The structure of atoms | 18 | | 36 | |
| Chemical equations and formulae | 18 | | 36 | |
| The mole | 18 | | 36 | |
| Chemical bonding and structure | 18 | | 36 | |
| Elements of groups 2 and 7 | 18 | | 36 | |
| The periodic table and periodicity | 18 | | 36 | |
| General questions | 18 | | 36 | |
| **Total** | **126** | | **252** | |
| **Organic chemistry** | | | | |
| Alkanes | 18 | | 36 | |
| Alkenes | 18 | | 36 | |
| Halogenoalkanes | 18 | | 36 | |
| Alcohols | 18 | | 36 | |
| General questions | 18 | | 36 | |
| **Total** | **90** | | **180** | |
| **Physical chemistry** | | | | |
| Enthalpy changes | 18 | | 36 | |
| Rates of reaction | 18 | | 36 | |
| Chemical equilibria and acids | 18 | | 36 | |
| General questions | 18 | | 36 | |
| **Total** | **72** | | **144** | |
| **OVERALL TOTAL** | **288** | | **576** | |

# Atoms, moles and the periodic table

# The structure of atoms

Questions 1–5 involve the following electronic configurations:

A $1s^2, 2s^2, 2p^4$
B $1s^2, 2s^2, 2p^6, 3s^2, 3p^6, 4s^2, 3d^{10}, 4p^6, 5s^1$
C $1s^2, 2s^2, 2p^6, 3s^2, 3p^6, 4s^2$
D $1s^2, 2s^2, 2p^6, 3s^2, 3p^6, 4s^2, 3d^6$
E $1s^2, 2s^2, 2p^6$

**1** Which of A–E is likely to have the lowest ionisation energy?

☐ A　　☐ B　　☐ C　　☐ D　　☐ E

What factors affect the magnitude of the ionisation energy?

......................................................................................................................................

......................................................................................................................................

......................................................................................................................................

**2** Which of A–E is likely to be an element that will form a chloride of general formula $XCl_2$, where X is the element?

☐ A　　☐ B　　☐ C　　☐ D　　☐ E

How is the group in which an element is likely to be found related to the electronic configuration?

......................................................................................................................................

......................................................................................................................................

......................................................................................................................................

**3** Which of A–E is likely to be an element that forms coloured compounds?

☐ A　　☐ B　　☐ C　　☐ D　　☐ E

Give an example of an element that is likely to form coloured compounds.

......................................................................................................................................

......................................................................................................................................

**4** Which of A–E is likely to be an element that forms an ion of charge –2?

☐ A　　☐ B　　☐ C　　☐ D　　☐ E

What is the likely formula of the compound formed between the answer to this and hydrogen?

......................................................................................................................................

......................................................................................................................................

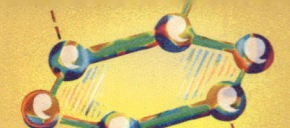

**5** Which of A–E is likely to be a noble gas?

        A        B        C        D        E

Why do helium, neon and argon not react with any other elements?

....................................................................................................................................................

....................................................................................................................................................

| Instructions for answering questions 6–18: | A 1, 2 and 3 only are correct<br>B 1 and 3 only are correct<br>C 2 and 4 only are correct<br>D 4 only is correct<br>E some other response |
| --- | --- |

**6** An ion has a mass number of 40 and has 19 protons in the nucleus. Select correct information about this ion from the following:
(1) it is found in group 2 of the periodic table
(2) it has 21 neutrons in the nucleus
(3) the element is in period 3 of the periodic table
(4) it is an isotope of an element

        A        B        C        D        E

What are isotopes?

....................................................................................................................................................

....................................................................................................................................................

....................................................................................................................................................

**7** The first six successive ionisation energies (in kJ mol$^{-1}$) in an element are: 577, 1820, 2740, 11 600, 14 800 and 18 400. From this information, it can be deduced that:
(1) the element could be sodium
(2) the next element in the periodic table would have a first ionisation energy greater than 577 kJ mol$^{-1}$
(3) the element is likely to form an ion of charge +2
(4) the element is in group 3

        A        B        C        D        E

How is the group in which an element is found related to its successive first ionisation energies?

....................................................................................................................................................

....................................................................................................................................................

....................................................................................................................................................

....................................................................................................................................................

**8** With reference to the two ions $^{12}_{6}C^+$ and $^{24}_{12}Mg^{2+}$, choose correct statements from the following:
(1) both ions would be deflected to different extents within a magnetic field in a mass spectrometer
(2) both ions are likely to have the same abundance
(3) both ions have the same number of neutrons
(4) both ions have the same mass-to-charge ratio

    A      B      C      D      E

What are the five main changes that take place in a sample within a mass spectrometer?

**9**

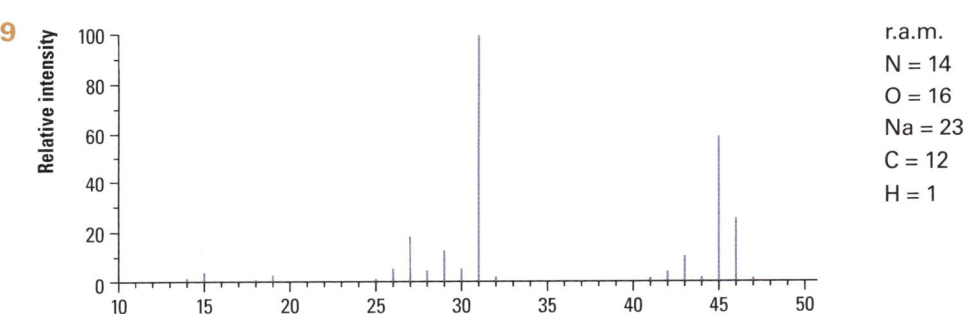

r.a.m.
N = 14
O = 16
Na = 23
C = 12
H = 1

Which of the following could have been responsible for the mass spectrum shown?
(1) nitrogen dioxide, $NO_2$
(2) 2 mol of sodium
(3) a mixture of the $^{12}C$, $^{13}C$ and $^{14}C$ isotopes of carbon
(4) ethanol, $C_2H_5OH$

    A      B      C      D      E

Why do most elements produce more than one peak in their mass spectrum?

**10** The electronic configuration $1s^2$, $2s^2$, $2p^6$, $3s^2$, $3p^6$, $3d^3$ could be due to:
(1) $Mn^{4+}$
(2) $V^{3+}$
(3) $Cr^{3+}$
(4) V
(Atomic number: Mn = 25; V = 23; Cr = 24)

    A      B      C      D      E

What do all transition metals have in common with regard to their electronic configurations?

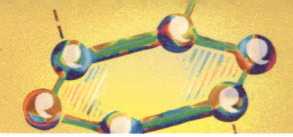

**11** An element has two atomic forms of mass numbers 10 and 11 and with relative abundances 18.7% and 81.3% respectively. From this information, it can be deduced that:

(1) both atomic forms are allotropes

(2) the average relative atomic mass is given by $(0.187 \times 10) + (0.813 \times 11)$

(3) the mass spectrum for the element would give a peak at $m/z = 5.5$

(4) both atomic forms are isotopes

A          B          C          D          E

What are allotropes?

....................................................................................................................................

....................................................................................................................................

Questions 12–15 refer to the following section taken from a first ionisation energy against atomic number plot.

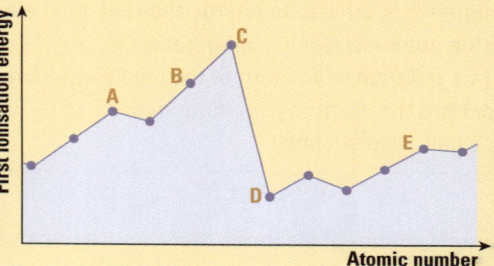

**12** From the graph, it can be deduced that:

(1) element C is in group 1

(2) elements A and E are in the same group of the periodic table

(3) element B has the outer electronic configuration $s^2$, $p^4$

(4) element E could form an oxide of empirical formula $E_2O_5$

A          B          C          D          E

Why does the first ionisation energy decrease down a group of the periodic table?

....................................................................................................................................

....................................................................................................................................

**13** Element C has a higher first ionisation energy than element B because:

(1) element B has a greater nuclear charge

(2) element C has a full outer shell of electrons

(3) element C has fewer protons

(4) element C has its outer electrons more tightly bound to the nucleus

A          B          C          D          E

In which group of the periodic table would C be placed?

....................................................................................................................................

....................................................................................................................................

**14** Element D has the lowest ionisation energy in the section shown in the graph. Reasons for this are that element D:

(1) has more protons

(2) is the least reactive of the elements in the section

(3) has the lowest charge density of the elements

(4) has its outer electron furthest from the nucleus

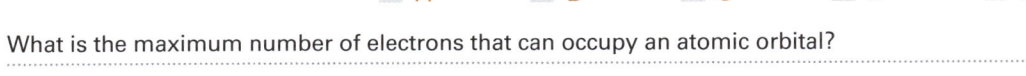   A        B        C        D        E

Why do group 1 metals become more reactive as the group is descended?

.............................................................................................................

.............................................................................................................

.............................................................................................................

**15** Element A has a higher first ionisation energy than the next element. Reasons for this include:

(1) element A has the outer electronic configuration $s^2$, $p^3$

(2) two electrons in a $p$-orbital in an atom of the next element repel each other

(3) the next element has the electronic configuration $s^2$, $p^4$

(4) element A has a half-filled subshell

  A        B        C        D        E

What is the maximum number of electrons that can occupy an atomic orbital?

.............................................................................................................

.............................................................................................................

Questions 16–18 refer to the following graph, which shows how atomic radius varies with atomic number for the first 36 elements.

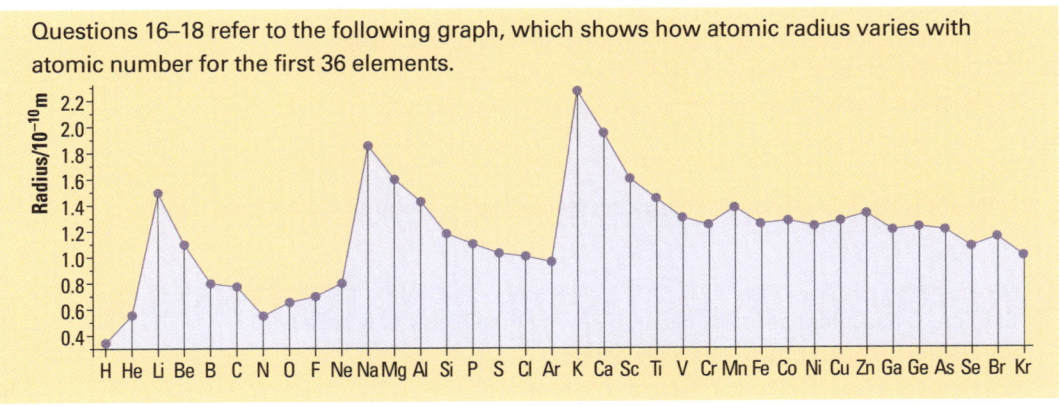

**16** From this graph, it can be deduced that:

(1) atomic radius decreases going down a group of the periodic table

(2) atomic radius generally decreases across a period, moving from left to right

(3) the largest atomic radius of all of the elements in the periodic table is that of potassium

(4) the variation of atomic radius with atomic number is an example of periodicity

  A        B        C        D        E

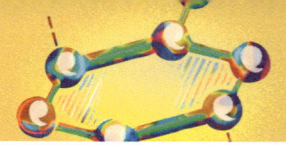

What is meant by the term 'periodicity'?

................................................................................................

................................................................................................

**17** Potassium has a larger atomic radius than argon because:
   (1) potassium has more protons in the nucleus
   (2) argon has fewer electron shells
   (3) potassium has a larger nucleus
   (4) the outer electron of potassium experiences a lesser attraction of the nuclear charge

   A      B      C      D      E

Why is argon less reactive than potassium?

................................................................................................

................................................................................................

................................................................................................

................................................................................................

**18** A lithium atom has a smaller atomic radius than sodium because:
   (1) sodium has more protons in its nucleus
   (2) a lithium atom has fewer electron shells
   (3) the outer electron in a sodium atom is attracted more towards the nucleus than the outer electron in a lithium atom
   (4) the outer lithium electron has less shielding from the inner electron shells

   A      B      C      D      E

What happens to the atomic radius when moving across a period of the periodic table from left to right?

................................................................................................

................................................................................................

................................................................................................

# Chemical equations and formulae

Questions 1–5 are concerned with the following:

A $KNO_3$
B $K_2Cr_2O_7$
C $C_3H_6$
D $C_5H_{12}$
E $KNO_2$

(Relevant information: sulphate(VI) ion, $SO_4^{2-}$; carbonate, $CO_3^{2-}$; nitrate(V), $NO_3^-$)

**1** Which of A–E is called potassium nitrate(III)?

         ■ A      ■ B      ■ C      ■ D      ■ E

What is the chemical formula of barium nitrate(III)?

.................................................................................................................................

.................................................................................................................................

**2** Which of A–E is called propene?

         ■ A      ■ B      ■ C      ■ D      ■ E

What is the empirical formula of propene?

.................................................................................................................................

.................................................................................................................................

**3** Which of A–E contains a metal in the oxidation state of +6?

         ■ A      ■ B      ■ C      ■ D      ■ E

Show your working.

.................................................................................................................................

.................................................................................................................................

.................................................................................................................................

.................................................................................................................................

**4** Which of A–E contains an element in the oxidation state of +5?

         ■ A      ■ B      ■ C      ■ D      ■ E

What is the oxidation number of manganese in $KMnO_4$?

.................................................................................................................................

.................................................................................................................................

**5** Which of A–E is called pentane?

         ■ A      ■ B      ■ C      ■ D      ■ E

Name a compound of molecular formula $C_7H_{16}$.

.................................................................................................................................

.................................................................................................................................

Instructions for answering questions 6–12:

A 1, 2 and 3 only are correct
B 1 and 3 only are correct
C 2 and 4 only are correct
D 4 only is correct
E some other response

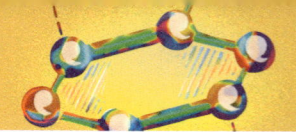

**6** Gallium is a metal found in group 3 of the periodic table. Choose correct statements from the following:

(1) compounds of gallium and a non-metal are likely to be made up of ions

(2) the formula of gallium chloride is likely to be $GaCl_3$

(3) gallium is likely to form an ion of formula $Ga^{3+}$

(4) the formula of gallium oxide is likely to be $Ga_3O_2$

    A        B        C        D        E

What is the chemical formula for gallium sulphate?

........................................................................................................................................

........................................................................................................................................

**7** The formula for hydrated copper(II) sulphate is $CuSO_4.5H_2O$. Choose correct statements from the following:

(1) the copper ion has a charge of +1

(2) 1 mol of $CuSO_4.5H_2O$ consists of 1 mol of $CuSO_4$ and 5 mol of $H_2O$

(3) the compound consists solely of ionic bonds

(4) the formula of anhydrous copper(I) sulphate is $Cu_2SO_4$

    A        B        C        D        E

What is observed when blue hydrated copper(II) sulphate is heated?

........................................................................................................................................

........................................................................................................................................

**8** Lead(IV) oxide reacts with concentrated hydrochloric acid according to the following equation:

$$PbO_2(s) + 4HCl(aq) \longrightarrow PbCl_2(s) + Cl_2(g) + 2H_2O(l)$$

Which of the following are *true* statements about the equation:

(1) the reaction is a redox reaction

(2) the lead compound produced is soluble in water

(3) one of the products is called lead(II) chloride

(4) the equation $2Cl^- + 2e^- \longrightarrow Cl_2$ describes accurately what happens to the chloride ion in this reaction

    A        B        C        D        E

What is meant by the term 'reduction'?

........................................................................................................................................

........................................................................................................................................

**9** When sodium reacts with fluorine, a new compound forms. It is true to say that:

(1) sodium is the reducing agent in the reaction

(2) the sodium has changed from an atom to an ion

(3) a fluorine molecule, $F_2$, has formed fluoride ions, $F^-$

(4) the equation for the reaction is $Na(s) + F_2(g) \longrightarrow NaF_2(s)$

    A        B        C        D        E

Define 'oxidising agent' in terms of electron transfer.

..........................................................................................................................................................................

..........................................................................................................................................................................

**10** Consider the compounds butane, decene and heptane and choose correct statements from the following:
(1) they are all alkenes
(2) they are all hydrocarbons
(3) all have the same empirical formula
(4) they have molecular formulae $C_4H_{10}$, $C_{10}H_{20}$ and $C_7H_{16}$ respectively

         A          B          C          D          E

What is meant by 'molecular formula'?

..........................................................................................................................................................................

..........................................................................................................................................................................

**11** 0.1 mol of a metal, M, reacts with 0.2 mol of solid iodine, $I_2$, to form a new compound. Choose correct statements from the following:
(1) 1 mol of the metal combines with 4 mol of iodine atoms
(2) the metal could be calcium
(3) the metal could be in group 4 of the periodic table
(4) the equation for the reaction could be $M(s) + 2I_2(s) \longrightarrow MI_4(s)$

         A          B          C          D          E

How many moles of oxygen atoms are present in 0.1 mol of ozone, $O_3$?

..........................................................................................................................................................................

..........................................................................................................................................................................

**12** Phosphorus reacts with copper(II) sulphate solution to yield copper metal, phosphoric(V) acid, $H_3PO_4$ and sulphuric(VI) acid. Choose correct statements from the following:
(1) the reaction is not a redox process
(2) the phosphorus has been reduced
(3) copper reacts according to the half equation $Cu^{2+} + 2e^- \longrightarrow Cu$
(4) the equation for the reaction is $2P + 5CuSO_4 + 8H_2O \longrightarrow 2H_3PO_4 + 5H_2SO_4 + 5Cu$

         A          B          C          D          E

Is phosphorus acting as an oxidising agent or as a reducing agent in the reaction?

..........................................................................................................................................................................

..........................................................................................................................................................................

**13** The correct formulae for anhydrous cobalt(II) sulphate and copper(II) nitrate(V)-3-water are:

     A $CoSO_4$ and $Cu_2NO_3.3H_2O$
     B $CoSO_4$ and $Cu(NO_3)_2$
     C $CoSO_4$ and $Cu(NO_3)_2.3H_2O$
     D $CoSO_4$ and $Cu_2NO_3$
     E $Co_2SO_4$ and $Cu(NO_3)_2.3H_2O$

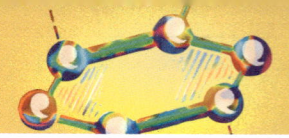

What is the formula for manganese(II) sulphate?

**14** Lead(II) nitrate decomposes on heating to form lead(II) oxide, nitrogen(IV) oxide and oxygen gas. A correct balanced equation for the reaction is:

   A $PbNO_3 \longrightarrow PbO + N + O_2$
   B $Pb(NO_3)_2 \longrightarrow PbO + 2NO + \frac{3}{2}O_2$
   C $PbNO_3 \longrightarrow PbO + NO + O$
   D $Pb(NO_3)_2 \longrightarrow PbO + 2NO_2 + O$
   E $2Pb(NO_3)_2 \longrightarrow 2PbO + 4NO_2 + O_2$

What is the formula for lead(II) carbonate?

**15** Lead(II) bromide is electrolysed to form lead and bromine gas. The correct half-equation for the process is:

   A $Pb^{2+} \longrightarrow Pb + 2e^-$
   B $Br^- + e^- \longrightarrow Br$
   C $Br_2 + 2e^- \longrightarrow 2Br^-$
   D $2Br^- \longrightarrow Br_2 + 2e^-$
   E $Pb^+ + e^- \longrightarrow Pb$

What chemical term describes the process occurring at the anode in this electrolysis?

**16** When nitric(V) acid is added to calcium carbonate, a reaction occurs in which calcium nitrate solution and two other products are formed. Which is an appropriate equation for this reaction?

   A $CaCO_3 + HNO_3 \longrightarrow$
        $CaNO_3 + CO_2 + \frac{1}{2}O_2$
   B $Ca^{2+} + 2e^- \longrightarrow Ca$
   C $CaCO_3 + 2H^+ \longrightarrow$
        $Ca^{2+} + H_2O + CO_2$
   D $2H^+ + 2e^- \longrightarrow H_2$
   E $H^+ + OH^- \longrightarrow H_2O$

Give an equation for the reaction between calcium oxide and dilute nitric acid.

**17** A metallic element X is found in group 3 of the periodic table and a non-metallic element is found in group 5. The likely formula of the compound formed between X and Y is:

   A $XY_3$
   B $XY_2$
   C $X_2Y$
   D $XY$
   E $X_2Y_3$

What is the formula of the compound formed when element X reacts with oxygen?

**18** The ionic equation for the reaction between copper(II) oxide and dilute sulphuric(VI) acid is:

    A $CuO + 2H^+ \longrightarrow Cu^{2+} + H_2O$
    B $H^+ + OH^- \longrightarrow H_2O$
    C $Cu^{2+} + 2e^- \longrightarrow Cu$
    D $Cu^{2+} \longrightarrow Cu + 2e^-$
    E $CuO \longrightarrow Cu^{2+} + O^{2-}$

What is the purpose of writing an ionic equation for a reaction?

# The mole

Questions 1–6 are concerned with the reaction that occurs when titanium(IV) oxide is heated with carbon and chlorine gas:

$TiO_2(s) + 2C(s) + 2Cl_2(g) \longrightarrow TiCl_4(l) + 2CO(g)$
(r.a.m. Ti = 48, C = 12, O = 16, Cl = 35.5)

**1** The mass (in g) of titanium(IV) chloride, $TiCl_4$, that should form when 20.0 g of titanium(IV) oxide is used is:

    A 760
    B 47.5
    C 190
    D 80
    E an alternative answer

Show your working.

**2** Which of the following will give the mass (in tonnes) of titanium(IV) oxide, $TiO_2$, that is required to form exactly 3.50 tonnes of titanium(IV) chloride, $TiCl_4$?

    A $3.50 \times (190/80)$
    B $3.50/190$
    C $3.50 \times (80/190)$
    D 3.50
    E an alternative answer

Show your working.

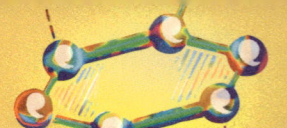

**3** The number of moles of chlorine gas, $Cl_2$, required to react with $5.0 \times 10^{-3}$ mol of titanium(IV) oxide is:

◻ A 0.5
◻ B 0.001
◻ C 2
◻ D 0.1
◻ E 0.01

Show your working.

**4** If 1.00 g each of titanium(IV) oxide, carbon and chlorine gas are heated, the expected mass (in g) of titanium(IV) chloride would be:

◻ A 1.33
◻ B 2.67
◻ C 15.8
◻ D 2.38
◻ E an alternative answer

Show your working.

**5** Which of the following will give the mass (in tonnes) of titanium that is expected when exactly 1.00 tonne of titanium(IV) chloride is reduced?

◻ A 48
◻ B 190/48
◻ C 1000/48
◻ D 48/190
◻ E an alternative answer

Show your working.

**6** In another experiment, the percentage yield of titanium(IV) chloride was 65.0%. If 2.00 g of titanium(IV) oxide was reacted, the mass (in g) of titanium(IV) chloride formed would be:

◻ A 3.09
◻ B 7.31
◻ C 4.75
◻ D 2.38
◻ E an alternative answer

Show your working.

Instructions for answering
questions 7–12:

A 1, 2 and 3 only are correct
B 1 and 3 only are correct
C 2 and 4 only are correct
D 4 only is correct
E some other response

**7** In most periodic tables, lithium is written as:

$$^{7}_{3}\text{Li}$$

(r.a.m. Li = 7)

Choose correct statements about lithium from the following:

(1) the mass number of lithium is 7
(2) there are seven neutrons present in a nucleus of a lithium atom
(3) 1.00 kg of lithium atoms would consist of approximately 140 mol
(4) the average relative atomic mass of lithium is exactly 7.000

    A        B        C        D        E

What is meant by the term 'relative atomic mass'?

......................................................................................................................................................................

......................................................................................................................................................................

......................................................................................................................................................................

**8** Separate samples of methane gas and helium gas were found to have the same volume under the same conditions of temperature and pressure. Choose correct statements from the following:

(1) the mass of gas must be the same for each
(2) the number of moles of gas must be the same for each
(3) the densities of the gases must be the same
(4) the gases must consist of the same number of molecules

    A        B        C        D        E

What happens to the density of a gas as temperature is increased at constant pressure?

......................................................................................................................................................................

......................................................................................................................................................................

**9** 20 cm³ of a hydrocarbon gas reacts with 70 cm³ of oxygen gas exactly, both volumes being measured under the same conditions of temperature and pressure. The hydrocarbon could be:

(1) methane
(2) propane
(3) ethene
(4) ethane

    A        B        C        D        E

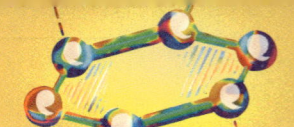

Show your working.

..................................................................................................................................

..................................................................................................................................

..................................................................................................................................

..................................................................................................................................

**10** $15\,cm^3$ of a gaseous hydrocarbon, $C_aH_b$, reacts with oxygen to form $60\,cm^3$ of carbon dioxide at $298\,K$. Which of the following statements could be deduced from this information?
(1) the hydrocarbon could be butane
(2) the volume of oxygen required is equal to $15(a + \frac{b}{4})\,cm^3$
(3) 1 mol of the hydrocarbon produces 4 mol of carbon dioxide
(4) if the hydrocarbon were butene, $60\,cm^3$ of liquid water would form

        A         B         C         D         E

What is the amount of gas present in $20.0\,cm^3$ of methane measured at room temperature and pressure?

..................................................................................................................................

..................................................................................................................................

**11** If $L$ is the Avogadro constant (the number of specified particles in 1 mol of a substance), then which of the following are true?
(1) the number of ions in 1 mol of NaCl is $L$
(2) the number of *atoms* in 11 g of carbon dioxide molecules is $0.75L$
(3) 2 mol of hydrogen molecules contains $2L$ hydrogen atoms
(4) the number of molecules in $9\,cm^3$ of liquid water is $0.5L$

        A         B         C         D         E

How many atoms are present in 0.1 mol of sulphuric acid, $H_2SO_4$?

..................................................................................................................................

..................................................................................................................................

**12** An oxide of sodium is found to contain 58.9% by mass of sodium. The molar mass of the compound is $78\,g\,mol^{-1}$. Which of the following are true?
(r.a.m. Na = 23, O = 16)
(1) the compound contains 41.1% oxygen by mass
(2) the empirical formula of the compound is NaO
(3) the molecular formula is $Na_2O_2$
(4) the compound is expected to be a good electrical conductor when solid

        A         B         C         D         E

What is meant by 'empirical formula'?

..................................................................................................................................

..................................................................................................................................

| Questions 13–17 are concerned with the following quantities: | A 11.2 g<br>B 1.00 g<br>C 0.33 g<br>D 4.50 g<br>E an alternative answer | (1 mol of any gas at room temperature and pressure will occupy 24 000 cm³; r.a.m. C = 12, O = 16, H = 1, K = 39, Cl = 35.5, Ca = 40, Zn = 65) |
|---|---|---|

**13** Which of A–E is the mass of carbon required to form 1.2 g of carbon dioxide on burning in a plentiful supply of oxygen?

    ▨ A      ▨ B      ▨ C      ▨ D      ▨ E

Show your working.

..........................................................................................................................................................

..........................................................................................................................................................

**14** Which of A–E is the mass of glucose ($C_6H_{12}O_6$) required to make 25 cm³ of a 1.0 mol dm⁻³ solution?

    ▨ A      ▨ B      ▨ C      ▨ D      ▨ E

Show your working.

..........................................................................................................................................................

..........................................................................................................................................................

**15** Which of A–E is the mass of potassium chloride that contains as many ions as there are ions in 0.1 mol of calcium chloride?

    ▨ A      ▨ B      ▨ C      ▨ D      ▨ E

Show your working.

..........................................................................................................................................................

..........................................................................................................................................................

..........................................................................................................................................................

**16** Which of A–E is the mass of zinc oxide that should form when 3.61 g of zinc is heated in oxygen, according to the equation $2Zn(s) + O_2(g) \longrightarrow 2ZnO(s)$?

    ▨ A      ▨ B      ▨ C      ▨ D      ▨ E

Show your working.

..........................................................................................................................................................

..........................................................................................................................................................

**17** Which of A–E is the mass of calcium carbonate that, when reacted with excess hydrochloric acid, will form 240 cm³ of carbon dioxide at room temperature and pressure?

    ▨ A      ▨ B      ▨ C      ▨ D      ▨ E

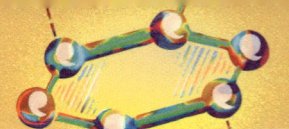

Show your working.

........................................................................................................

........................................................................................................

**18** In an experiment to determine the concentration of sodium hydroxide solution, 25.0 cm$^3$ of sodium hydroxide solution was titrated with sulphuric acid of concentration 0.35 mol dm$^{-3}$. It was found that 22.30 cm$^3$ of sulphuric acid was required for neutralisation.

The formulae of the products of this reaction are:

A $NaSO_4$ and $H_2O$
B $Na_2SO_4 + H_2$
C $Na_2SO_4$ and $H_2O$
D $NaSO_4 + O_2$
E $Na_2SO_4$ only

Write an equation for this reaction.

........................................................................................................

........................................................................................................

# Chemical bonding and structure

Instructions for answering questions 1–4:

A 1, 2 and 3 only are correct
B 1 and 3 only are correct
C 2 and 4 only are correct
D 4 only is correct
E some other response

Consider the following:

(1) Si
(2) NaCl
(3) $NH_4Cl$
(4) $CO_2$

**1** Which of the above has/have a simple covalent structure?

A          B          C          D          E

Describe what is meant by 'simple covalent structure'.

........................................................................................................

........................................................................................................

**2** Which of the above contain(s) dative bonds?

A          B          C          D          E

How does a dative bond form?

.................................................................................................................................

.................................................................................................................................

.................................................................................................................................

.................................................................................................................................

**3** Which of the above form(s) a giant structure?

▨ A          ▨ B          ▨ C          ▨ D          ▨ E

What is meant by 'giant structure'?

.................................................................................................................................

.................................................................................................................................

**4** Which of the above consist(s) of linear molecules?

▨ A          ▨ B          ▨ C          ▨ D          ▨ E

What is the shape of the molecule having the formula HOCl?

.................................................................................................................................

.................................................................................................................................

| Questions 5–10 are concerned with the following three-dimensional shapes: | A tetrahedral<br>B trigonal pyramidal<br>C linear<br>D trigonal planar<br>E non-linear |
|---|---|

**5** Which of A–E is the shape of $CH_4$ molecules?

▨ A          ▨ B          ▨ C          ▨ D          ▨ E

What is the internal angle in a molecule of methane?

.................................................................................................................................

.................................................................................................................................

**6** Which of A–E is the shape of $BF_3$ molecules?

▨ A          ▨ B          ▨ C          ▨ D          ▨ E

Does this molecule have an overall dipole moment?

.................................................................................................................................

.................................................................................................................................

**7** Which of A–E is the shape of $NH_3$ molecules?

▨ A          ▨ B          ▨ C          ▨ D          ▨ E

What is the internal angle in an ammonia molecule?

.................................................................................................................................

.................................................................................................................................

**8** Which of A–E is the shape of HCN molecules?

           ☒ A         ☒ B         ☒ C         ☒ D         ☒ E

Does this molecule have an overall dipole moment?

.................................................................................................................................

.................................................................................................................................

**9** Which of A–E is the shape of the $CO_3^{2-}$ ion?

           ☒ A         ☒ B         ☒ C         ☒ D         ☒ E

Suggest why all of the bonds in the carbonate ion are the same length.

.................................................................................................................................

.................................................................................................................................

**10** Which of A–E is the shape of the $NO_3^-$ ion?

           ☒ A         ☒ B         ☒ C         ☒ D         ☒ E

What is the expected shape of the nitrate(III) ion, $NO_2^-$?

.................................................................................................................................

.................................................................................................................................

| Instructions for answering questions 11–18: | A 1, 2 and 3 only are correct<br>B 1 and 3 only are correct<br>C 2 and 4 only are correct<br>D 4 only is correct<br>E some other response |
|---|---|

**11** Calcium oxide conducts electricity in the molten state because:
  (1) calcium is a metal and all metals are good electrical conductors
  (2) mobile electrons are present
  (3) $Ca^+$ and $O^-$ ions are present
  (4) ions are able to move

           ☒ A         ☒ B         ☒ C         ☒ D         ☒ E

What would be an appropriate question if the answer were 'because electrons are free to move and can carry the charge'?

.................................................................................................................................

.................................................................................................................................

.................................................................................................................................

**12** The bonding in lithium iodide is not 100% ionic. Relevant information that could explain this type of bonding includes:

(1) lithium ions have a high charge density

(2) lithium and iodine atoms attract each other using van der Waals interactions

(3) iodide ions have a large ionic radius

(4) lithium ions are small and so can be polarised by the large iodide ions

▨ A          ▨ B          ▨ C          ▨ D          ▨ E

Is lithium iodide more, or less, covalent than lithium fluoride? Explain your answer.

**13** Correct statements about this giant ionic structure include:

(1) the smaller ions are normally cations

(2) the substance could be sodium chloride

(3) the ions are attracted to each other electrostatically

(4) it is made up of molecules

▨ A          ▨ B          ▨ C          ▨ D          ▨ E

Why do ionic structures generally have high melting temperatures?

**14** This molecule is called buckminsterfullerene and it has the formula $C_{60}$. Correct statements about this molecule include:

(1) it consists of 60 atoms bonded together covalently

(2) each carbon atom is bonded to three others

(3) the molecule is likely to be soluble in non-polar solvents

(4) the substance is likely to be soluble in water

▨ A          ▨ B          ▨ C          ▨ D          ▨ E

What type of structure is $C_{60}$ expected to possess?

Questions 15–17 are concerned with the following substances and their boiling points:

| Choice | Substance | Formula | Boiling point/°C |
|---|---|---|---|
| (1) | Hydrogen fluoride | HF | 20 |
| (2) | Propanone | $CH_3COCH_3$ | 56 |
| (3) | Ethanol | $C_2H_5OH$ | 79 |
| (4) | Hexane | $C_6H_{12}$ | 69 |

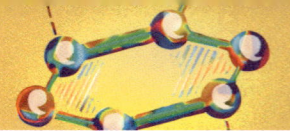

**15** In which substances is hydrogen bonding the dominant intermolecular force?

          A          B          C          D          E

What is so special about hydrogen in a hydrogen bond?

.................................................................................................................................................

.................................................................................................................................................

.................................................................................................................................................

.................................................................................................................................................

**16** In which substances are van der Waals forces the dominant intermolecular force?

          A          B          C          D          E

How does a van der Waals force arise between two molecules?

.................................................................................................................................................

.................................................................................................................................................

.................................................................................................................................................

**17** In which substances are dipole–dipole interactions the dominant intermolecular force?

          A          B          C          D          E

What is meant by a dipole?

.................................................................................................................................................

.................................................................................................................................................

.................................................................................................................................................

**18** Which of the following substances should be very soluble in water?

(1) $C_2H_5OH$

(2) $N_2$

(3) $C_6H_{12}O_6$

(4) $C_6H_{14}$

          A          B          C          D          E

Why are polar substances more soluble in water than in non-polar solvents?

.................................................................................................................................................

.................................................................................................................................................

.................................................................................................................................................

.................................................................................................................................................

# Elements of groups 2 and 7

Questions 1–5 refer to the following compounds:

A potassium chloride
B potassium bromide
C silver(I) iodide
D calcium carbonate
E silver(I) chloride

**1** Which of A–E reacts with a solution of silver(I) nitrate solution to form a white precipitate?

⬜ A  ⬜ B  ⬜ C  ⬜ D  ⬜ E

Write an ionic equation for this reaction.

.............................................................................................................................................................

.............................................................................................................................................................

**2** Which of A–E forms an orange solution when chlorine gas is bubbled through it?

⬜ A  ⬜ B  ⬜ C  ⬜ D  ⬜ E

What is the name for this type of reaction?

.............................................................................................................................................................

.............................................................................................................................................................

**3** Select the halide that does not dissolve in either dilute or concentrated ammonia solution.

⬜ A  ⬜ B  ⬜ C  ⬜ D  ⬜ E

Describe a chemical test to distinguish between sodium chloride solution and sodium iodide solution.

.............................................................................................................................................................

.............................................................................................................................................................

.............................................................................................................................................................

.............................................................................................................................................................

**4** Which of A–E decomposes on heating, producing a gas that turns limewater milky?

⬜ A  ⬜ B  ⬜ C  ⬜ D  ⬜ E

What is the name of the suspension formed when limewater goes milky?

.............................................................................................................................................................

.............................................................................................................................................................

**5** Which of A–E has the greatest degree of ionic bonding?

⬜ A  ⬜ B  ⬜ C  ⬜ D  ⬜ E

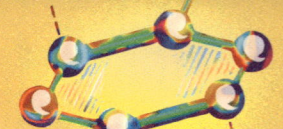

What factors determine the degree of ionic bonding in a compound?

Question 6–11 relate to the following reaction scheme:
When calcium carbonate is heated strongly, a white solid A and a colourless gas B are formed. If excess water is then added to solid A, a colourless solution C is formed. When carbon dioxide gas is passed through solution C, a white suspension D is formed. Continued passage of carbon dioxide gas through suspension D results in a colourless solution E. When E is heated, a white suspension is formed. On adding dilute hydrochloric acid to solution C, a reaction occurs, producing F.

**6** The formula of the metal-containing species in solution E is:

- A $CaO$
- B $Ca(OH)_2$
- C $Ca(HCO_3)_2$
- D $CaCO_3$
- E $Ca$

Write down the formulae of the ions that constitute solution E.

**7** How many stages in the description above involve redox reactions?

- A 4
- B 3
- C 2
- D 1
- E 0

A reaction occurs when sodium is added to water. Is it a redox reaction? Explain your answer.

**8** The type of reaction that occurs when carbon dioxide is bubbled through solution C to form D is:

- A displacement
- B oxidation
- C neutralisation
- D reduction
- E decomposition

What will happen to the electrical conductivity of solution C when suspension D is forming?

**9** The formula of the metal-containing product F is:

- ☒ A CaCl
- ☒ B $Ca(OCl)_2$
- ☒ C $Ca(OH)_2$
- ☒ D $CaCl_2$
- ☒ E $CaCO_3$

What is the formula for calcium sulphate?

.........................................................................................................

.........................................................................................................

**10** The ionic equation for the reaction taking place in forming product F is:

- ☒ A $HCO_3^- + H^+ \longrightarrow H_2O + CO_2$
- ☒ B $H_2O \longrightarrow H^+ + OH^-$
- ☒ C $Ca \longrightarrow Ca^{2+} + 2e^-$
- ☒ D $H^+ + OH^- \longrightarrow H_2O$
- ☒ E $CaCO_3 + 2H^+ \longrightarrow Ca^{2+} + CO_2 + H_2O$

Write an ionic equation for the reaction that takes place when calcium reacts with dilute hydrochloric acid.

.........................................................................................................

.........................................................................................................

**11** If exactly 1.00 g of calcium carbonate is heated in an experiment, what mass of gas (in g) is expected to form? (r.a.m. Ca = 40, C = 12, O = 16)

- ☒ A 44
- ☒ B 100
- ☒ C 0.56
- ☒ D 0.50
- ☒ E 0.44

Show your working.

.........................................................................................................

.........................................................................................................

Questions 12–16 involve the following:

- A $Cl^-$
- B $Br_2$
- C $Br^-$
- D $F_2$
- E $I^-$

**12** Which of A–E is the most powerful reducing agent?

☒ A      ☒ B      ☒ C      ☒ D      ☒ E

What is a reducing agent, in terms of electron transfer?

.........................................................................................................

.........................................................................................................

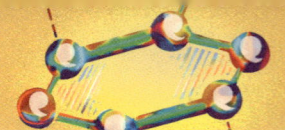

**13** Which of A–E is an ion that forms a yellow precipitate with silver(I) nitrate solution?

◾ A      ◾ B      ◾ C      ◾ D      ◾ E

What is meant by the term 'anion'?

................................................................................................................................

................................................................................................................................

**14** Which of A–E is the most powerful oxidising agent?

◾ A      ◾ B      ◾ C      ◾ D      ◾ E

What determines the strength of an oxidising agent?

................................................................................................................................

................................................................................................................................

**15** Which of A–E is the ion with the most endothermic ionisation energy?

◾ A      ◾ B      ◾ C      ◾ D      ◾ E

Comment on the endothermic nature of the ionisation energy of the astatide ion, $At^-$.

................................................................................................................................

................................................................................................................................

................................................................................................................................

................................................................................................................................

**16** Which of A–E has the smallest ionic radius?

◾ A      ◾ B      ◾ C      ◾ D      ◾ E

For a particular element, which has the smaller ionic radius: its cationic or anionic form?

................................................................................................................................

................................................................................................................................

| Instructions for answering questions 17–18: | A 1, 2 and 3 only are correct |
|---|---|
| | B 1 and 3 only are correct |
| | C 2 and 4 only are correct |
| | D 4 only is correct |
| | E some other response |

**17** Correct statements about iodide and chloride ions are:

(1) both are cations

(2) both are anions

(3) a chloride ion has a larger ionic radius than an iodide ion

(4) chloride ions are harder to oxidise than iodide ions

◾ A      ◾ B      ◾ C      ◾ D      ◾ E

Which of the ions would be expected to be more easily polarised? Explain your answer.

...................................................................................................................................................

...................................................................................................................................................

...................................................................................................................................................

**18** Lithium chloride and sodium bromide solutions can be distinguished by:
(1) adding dilute ammonia solution only
(2) bubbling through chlorine gas
(3) measuring electrical conductivity in the solid state
(4) adding silver(I) nitrate solution

     A       B       C       D       E

Write chemical equations for the reactions taking place.

...................................................................................................................................................

...................................................................................................................................................

...................................................................................................................................................

...................................................................................................................................................

# The periodic table and periodicity

Questions 1–6 refer to the periodic table shown.

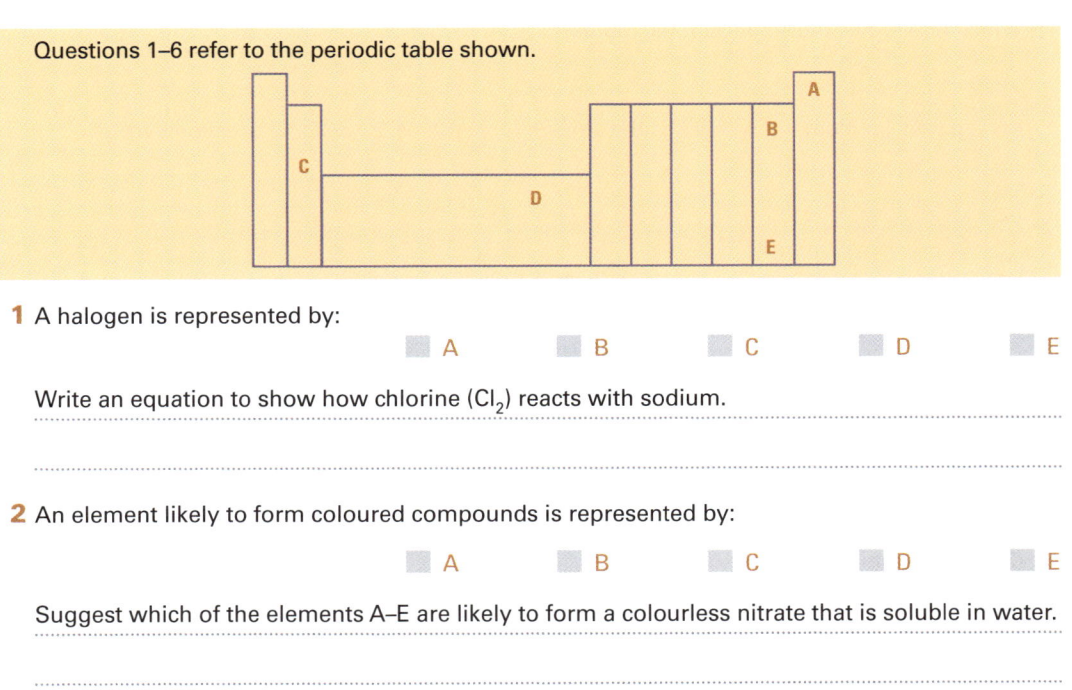

**1** A halogen is represented by:

     A       B       C       D       E

Write an equation to show how chlorine ($Cl_2$) reacts with sodium.

...................................................................................................................................................

...................................................................................................................................................

**2** An element likely to form coloured compounds is represented by:

     A       B       C       D       E

Suggest which of the elements A–E are likely to form a colourless nitrate that is soluble in water.

...................................................................................................................................................

...................................................................................................................................................

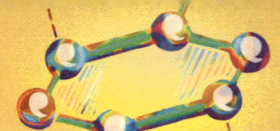

**3** The element with the highest first ionisation energy is represented by:

▨ A          ▨ B          ▨ C          ▨ D          ▨ E

Why does the first ionisation energy decrease on descending a group of the periodic table?

..................................................................................................................................................

..................................................................................................................................................

..................................................................................................................................................

**4** The element that, as a cation with a single positive charge, is the strongest oxidising agent is represented by:

▨ A          ▨ B          ▨ C          ▨ D          ▨ E

Write an equation that shows the first ionisation for this particular element.

..................................................................................................................................................

..................................................................................................................................................

**5** The element whose atoms are likely to have the largest atomic radius is represented by:

▨ A          ▨ B          ▨ C          ▨ D          ▨ E

What is the link, if any, between the magnitude of the atomic radius and first ionisation energy? Explain.

..................................................................................................................................................

..................................................................................................................................................

..................................................................................................................................................

..................................................................................................................................................

**6** A metal likely to show a range of oxidation states in its compounds is represented by:

▨ A          ▨ B          ▨ C          ▨ D          ▨ E

What is the oxidation state of nitrogen in ammonia?

..................................................................................................................................................

..................................................................................................................................................

| Instructions for answering questions 7–16: | A 1, 2 and 3 only are correct |
|---|---|
| | B 1 and 3 only are correct |
| | C 2 and 4 only are correct |
| | D 4 only is correct |
| | E some other response |

**7** True statements about group 1 elements include:
(1) they are all reactive metals
(2) the radius of the +1 ion increases as the group is descended
(3) they all react by losing their outer electron
(4) most of their compounds are insoluble in water

A      B      C      D      E

What is seen at the cathode when a solution containing a group 1 compound is electrolysed with graphite electrodes?

...........................................................................................................................

...........................................................................................................................

**8** When a group 2 metal reacts with water, which of the following statements is/are *true*?
(1) oxygen is formed
(2) hydrogen is formed
(3) a metal hydroxide of general formula MOH is formed, where M is the metal
(4) the metal atom is being oxidised in the reaction

A      B      C      D      E

Write an equation to show the reaction between magnesium and dilute sulphuric acid.

...........................................................................................................................

...........................................................................................................................

**9** Relevant statements in explaining the variation in electronegativity on moving from left to right across period 3 of the periodic table include:
(1) there are more electron shells
(2) there is a greater nuclear charge
(3) there is less shielding
(4) electrons are in the same electron shell

A      B      C      D      E

Define electronegativity.

...........................................................................................................................

...........................................................................................................................

...........................................................................................................................

**10** True statements about the reaction between lithium and iodine include:
(1) a compound forms that has the formula LiI
(2) the compound formed is ionic with appreciable covalent character
(3) the lithium atom is oxidised in the reaction
(4) the product forms a white precipitate with silver(I) nitrate solution

A      B      C      D      E

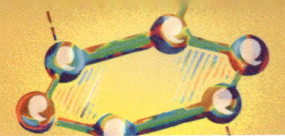

Write an equation for the reaction between lithium and iodine.

**11** In which of the following cases do boiling points increase?

(1) Li, Na, K

(2) $F_2$, $Cl_2$, $Br_2$

(3) $S_8$, $Cl_2$, Ar

(4) Na, Mg, Al

☐ A    ☐ B    ☐ C    ☐ D    ☐ E

Explain why helium has a lower boiling point than krypton.

**12** Which of the following statements about sodium chloride is/are *true*?

(1) it is an ionic compound

(2) it consists of $Na^-$ and $Cl^+$ ions

(3) its high boiling point can be explained in terms of electrostatic interactions between ions

(4) its electrical conductivity when molten can be explained in terms of moving electrons

☐ A    ☐ B    ☐ C    ☐ D    ☐ E

Explain why sodium chloride is soluble in water?

Questions 13–16 relate to the following pairs of elements:

(1) sodium and potassium

(2) sulphur and oxygen

(3) magnesium and calcium

(4) nitrogen and phosphorus

**13** Select the pair(s) of elements that has/have the outer electronic configuration $ns^2$, $np^3$, where $n$ is the shell number.

☐ A    ☐ B    ☐ C    ☐ D    ☐ E

In which group of the periodic table do these elements occur?

**14** Select the pair(s) of elements in which the first element has a higher boiling point than the second.

                         A           B           C           D           E

Does methane or ethane have the higher boiling point? Explain your answer.

.................................................................................................................................

.................................................................................................................................

.................................................................................................................................

.................................................................................................................................

**15** Select the pair(s) of elements in which the first element has the higher first ionisation energy.

                         A           B           C           D           E

Write an equation for the second ionisation of oxygen.

.................................................................................................................................

.................................................................................................................................

**16** Select the pair(s) of elements that have different boiling points that can be partly explained in terms of van der Waals interactions.

                         A           B           C           D           E

What factors determine the strength of van der Waals forces?

.................................................................................................................................

.................................................................................................................................

Questions 17–18 refer to the following graphs, in which the x-axis represents the atomic number for a period 2 element.

**17** In which of A–E does the y-axis represent the first ionisation energy?

                         A           B           C           D           E

Which elements form the peaks in the graph of first ionisation energy versus atomic number when many elements are plotted?

.................................................................................................................................

.................................................................................................................................

**18** In which of A–E does the y-axis represent atomic radius?

                         A           B           C           D           E

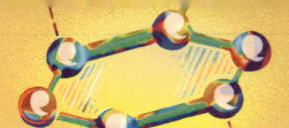

Which has the larger atomic radius, sodium or magnesium?

..................................................................................................................................................

..................................................................................................................................................

# General questions

Questions 1–5 refer to the
following types of reaction:

A displacement
B precipitation
C combustion
D neutralisation
E disproportionation

**1**   $Cl_2(g) + 2NaI(aq) \longrightarrow 2NaCl(aq) + I_2(aq)$
The reaction type for this process is:

▨ A          ▨ B          ▨ C          ▨ D          ▨ E

Convert this chemical equation to an ionic equation.
..................................................................................................................................................

..................................................................................................................................................

**2**   $2Mg(s) + O_2(g) \longrightarrow 2MgO(s)$
The reaction type for this process is:

▨ A          ▨ B          ▨ C          ▨ D          ▨ E

In terms of electron transfer, what has happened to the magnesium atom in this reaction?
..................................................................................................................................................

..................................................................................................................................................

**3**   $Ca(OH)_2(aq) + 2HCl(aq) \longrightarrow CaCl_2(aq) + 2H_2O(l)$
The reaction type for this process is:

▨ A          ▨ B          ▨ C          ▨ D          ▨ E

Convert this chemical equation to an ionic equation.
..................................................................................................................................................

..................................................................................................................................................

**4**   $2NaOH(aq) + Cl_2(g) \longrightarrow NaCl(aq) + NaOCl(aq) + H_2O(l)$
The reaction type for this process is:

▨ A          ▨ B          ▨ C          ▨ D          ▨ E

Give the oxidation numbers for chlorine before and after this reaction.
..................................................................................................................................................

..................................................................................................................................................

**5**  $NaBr(aq) + AgNO_3(aq) \longrightarrow AgBr(s) + NaNO_3(aq)$
The reaction type for this process is:

◪ A        ◪ B        ◪ C        ◪ D        ◪ E

Is this a redox reaction? Explain your answer.

................................................................................................................................

................................................................................................................................

................................................................................................................................

................................................................................................................................

Instructions for answering
questions 6–12:

A 1, 2 and 3 only are correct
B 1 and 3 only are correct
C 2 and 4 only are correct
D 4 only is correct
E some other response

**6** Correct statements about methylamine ($CH_3NH_2$) include:
(1)  the value for the H–N–H bond angle is approximately 107°
(2)  the molecule could form a dative bond with a proton
(3)  the molecular formula of the compound is $CH_5N$
(4)  the value for the H–C–H bond angle is 90°

▨ A        ▨ B        ▨ C        ▨ D        ▨ E

What is the % by mass of nitrogen in the compound? (r.a.m. C = 12, H = 1, N = 14)

................................................................................................................................

................................................................................................................................

**7** Chlorine gas reacts with magnesium according to the equation:
   $Mg(s) + Cl_2(g) \longrightarrow MgCl_2(s)$
(r.a.m. Mg = 24, Cl = 35.5)

Correct statements about this reaction include:
(1)  magnesium is reduced in the reaction
(2)  it is a redox reaction
(3)  1.00 g of magnesium should form 24/95 g of magnesium chloride
(4)  an aqueous solution of the product could form a white precipitate with silver(I) nitrate
   solution

▨ A        ▨ B        ▨ C        ▨ D        ▨ E

What is the name for the chemical structure adopted by $MgCl_2(s)$?

................................................................................................................................

................................................................................................................................

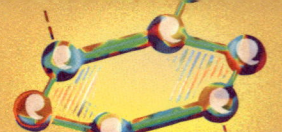

**8**

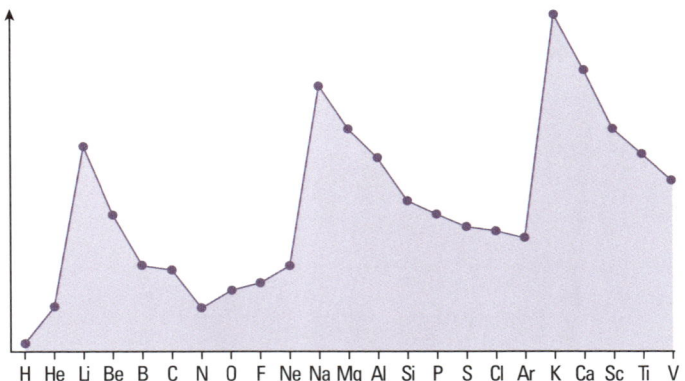

Correct statements about this graph section include:

(1) it shows periodicity
(2) it shows how first ionisation energy varies with atomic number
(3) it shows how atomic radius varies with atomic number
(4) it shows how electronegativity varies with atomic number

◼ A          ◼ B          ◼ C          ◼ D          ◼ E

Which has the greater ionic radius, $Na^+$ or $Mg^{2+}$? Explain your answer.

..................................................................................................................................

..................................................................................................................................

..................................................................................................................................

**9** True statements about the reaction between potassium and iodine include:

(1) the removal of an electron from potassium is exothermic
(2) iodine is oxidised in the reaction
(3) the equation for the reaction is $K(s) + I(s) \longrightarrow KI(s)$
(4) the compound formed consists of ions

◼ A          ◼ B          ◼ C          ◼ D          ◼ E

Would the product of the reaction have a high or a low melting point? Explain your answer.
..................................................................................................................................

..................................................................................................................................

**10** Which of the following can form a dative bond with boron trifluoride, $BF_3$?

(1) $F^-$
(2) $H_2O$
(3) $NH_3$
(4) $CH_4$

◼ A          ◼ B          ◼ C          ◼ D          ◼ E

What are the essential requirements for dative bond formation?

.................................................................................................................................................

.................................................................................................................................................

.................................................................................................................................................

**11** Study the mass spectrum for the element gallium, which has an atomic number of 31.

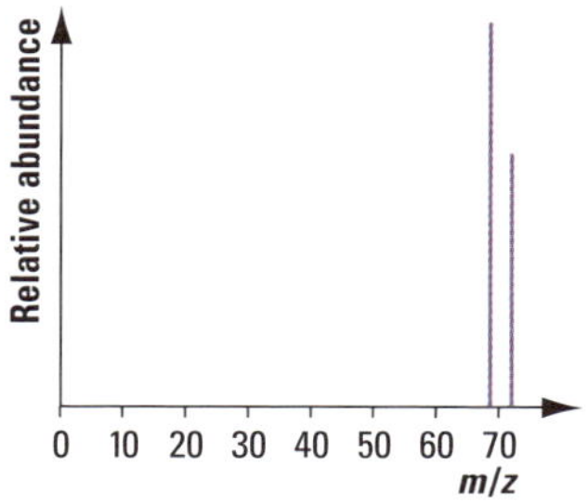

Which of the following statements are true?
(1) gallium has two isotopes
(2) only negative ions are formed in a mass spectrometer
(3) the detected ions could be $^{71}_{31}Ga^+$ and $^{69}_{31}Ga^+$
(4) the average relative atomic mass of gallium is closer to 71 than to 69

A     B     C     D     E

Write an equation to show the first ionisation of gallium.

.................................................................................................................................................

.................................................................................................................................................

**12** True statements about the orbitals include: 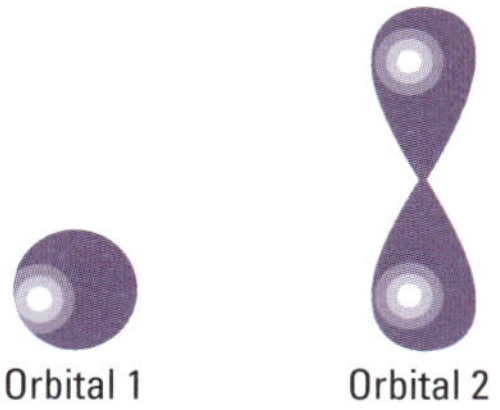
(1) orbital 1 is an $s$-orbital and orbital 2 is a $p$-orbital
(2) within a particular shell, orbital 1 is higher in energy than orbital 2
(3) an orbital is a region in space in which there is a high probability of an electron being found
(4) the second electron shell consists of one orbital 1 and four orbital 2s

Orbital 1      Orbital 2

A     B     C     D     E

Write down the electronic configuration for a potassium atom (atomic number 19).

.................................................................................................................................................

.................................................................................................................................................

**13** The correct order of increasing internal bond angles (smallest first) is:

A $CO_2$, $NH_3$, $H_2O$, $BF_3$, $CH_4$
B $BF_3$, $CH_4$, $H_2O$, $NH_3$, $CO_2$
C $CO_2$, $H_2O$, $CH_4$, $BF_3$, $NH_3$
D $NH_3$, $CH_4$, $BF_3$, $CO_2$, $H_2O$
E $H_2O$, $NH_3$, $CH_4$, $BF_3$, $CO_2$

What is the internal bond angle in the molecule $CF_4$?

.................................................................................................................................................

.................................................................................................................................................

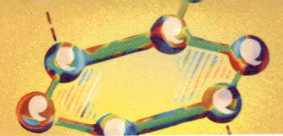

**14** Which of A–E consists of the greater number of specified particles?
(r.a.m. H = 1, O = 16, S = 32, He = 4; atomic number of He = 2; 1 mol of any gas occupies 24 000 cm$^3$, measured at room temperature and pressure)

- A molecules in 1 cm$^3$ of liquid water
- B ions in 1 cm$^3$ of 1.0 mol dm$^{-3}$ NaCl(aq)
- C molecules in 10 cm$^3$ of methane gas measured at room temperature and pressure
- D atoms in 1 g of sulphuric acid, H$_2$SO$_4$
- E protons in 1 g of helium

Show your working.

......................................................................................................

......................................................................................................

**15** The compound represented by the formula NaOCl:

- A is called sodium chloride
- B contains chlorine in the oxidation state −1
- C consists of the ions Na$^+$, O$^{2-}$ and Cl$^+$
- D could be made by bubbling chlorine through sodium hydroxide solution
- E is likely to be a coloured compound

Would NaOCl be expected to have a high melting temperature? Explain your answer.

......................................................................................................

......................................................................................................

......................................................................................................

......................................................................................................

**16** Which of A–E is equal to the Avogadro constant, 6.02 × 10$^{23}$ mol$^{-1}$?
(r.a.m. O = 16, C = 12)

- A the number of atoms in 32 g of oxygen gas, O$_2$
- B the number of ions in 1000 cm$^3$ of KCl(aq) of concentration 1.00 mol dm$^{-3}$
- C the number of molecules in 24 000 cm$^3$ of hydrogen gas measured at room temperature and pressure
- D 6 g of $^{12}_{6}$C
- E the number of atoms in 44 g of CO$_2$(g)

Show your working.

......................................................................................................

......................................................................................................

**17** Which of A–E represents the second ionisation energy of strontium?

- A Sr(s) $\longrightarrow$ Sr$^{2+}$(s) + 2e$^-$
- B Sr$^+$(s) $\longrightarrow$ Sr$^{2+}$(g) + e$^-$
- C Sr$^{2+}$(g) + e$^-$ $\longrightarrow$ Sr$^+$(g)
- D Sr$^+$(g) $\longrightarrow$ Sr$^{2+}$(g) + e$^-$
- E Sr(g) $\longrightarrow$ Sr$^{2+}$(g) + 2e$^-$

Will the first ionisation energy of strontium be higher or lower than that of magnesium? Explain your answer.

.................................................................................................................................

.................................................................................................................................

.................................................................................................................................

.................................................................................................................................

**18** Refer to the periodic table shown.

The element likely to be the most powerful oxidising agent is represented by:

A          B          C          D          E

Is the element sodium likely to behave as an oxidising agent under normal conditions? Explain your answer.

.................................................................................................................................

.................................................................................................................................

# Organic chemistry

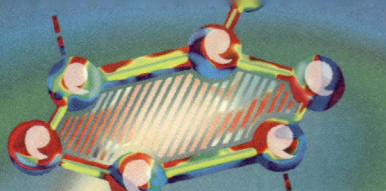

## Alkanes

Questions 1–5 relate to the alkanes shown.

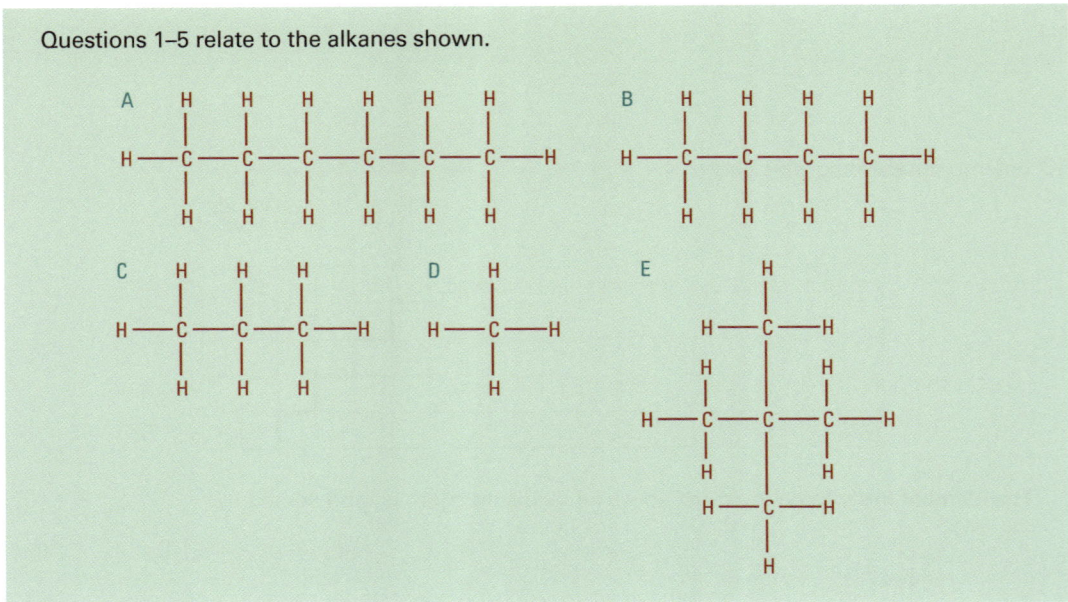

**1** Which of A–E is a structural isomer of *n*-pentane?

    A        B        C        D        E

How many structural isomers are there with the molecular formula $C_6H_{14}$?

**2** Which of A–E is likely to have the highest boiling point?

    A        B        C        D        E

What is the link between relative molecular mass and boiling point for non-polar molecules?

**3** 100 cm³ of which gaseous alkane reacts with exactly 200 cm³ of oxygen gas to form carbon dioxide and water?

    A        B        C        D        E

100 cm$^3$ of a gaseous alkane reacts with exactly 500 cm$^3$ of oxygen gas. How many carbon atoms are in the molecule of the alkane?

......................................................................................................................................

......................................................................................................................................

**4** Which of A–E has the empirical formula C$_2$H$_5$?

           ▨ A       ▨ B       ▨ C       ▨ D       ▨ E

Which alkane has an empirical formula of CH$_2$ and a molecular mass of 84?

......................................................................................................................................

......................................................................................................................................

**5** Which of A–E contains the greatest percentage of carbon by mass? (r.a.m. C = 12, H = 1)

           ▨ A       ▨ B       ▨ C       ▨ D       ▨ E

What is the percentage by mass of carbon in methane?

......................................................................................................................................

......................................................................................................................................

**6** The name of the molecule shown is:

   ▨ A 1-methyl-3-ethylhexane
   ▨ B 4-ethylhexane
   ▨ C 4-propylhexane
   ▨ D 4-ethylheptane
   ▨ E 4,4-dimethylheptane

What is the structural formula of 2,3-dimethylpentane.

......................................................................................................................................

......................................................................................................................................

**7** A mixture of butane and chlorine is exposed to ultraviolet light. How many different structural isomers are possible that contain two chlorine atoms per molecule? (Assume that the product contains four carbon atoms in a straight chain.)

   ▨ A 2
   ▨ B 3
   ▨ C 4
   ▨ D 5
   ▨ E 6

What are structural isomers?

......................................................................................................................................

......................................................................................................................................

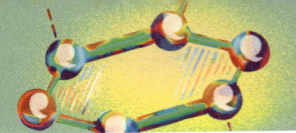

**8** $C_2H_6(g) + Cl_2(g) \longrightarrow C_2H_5Cl(g) + HCl(g)$
(Relevant bond energies (in kJ mol$^{-1}$): Cl–Cl = 242;
C–H = 412; C–C = 348; H–Cl = 431; C–Cl = 338)

A likely value for the enthalpy change for the reaction is:

◻ A +115
◻ B + 38
◻ C –115
◻ D –121
◻ E none of the above

Show your working.

.................................................................................................................................

.................................................................................................................................

Questions 9–11 are concerned with the reaction between methane gas and bromine vapour in the presence of ultraviolet light.

**9** The name of the mechanism for this reaction is:

◻ A combustion
◻ B oxidation
◻ C radical addition
◻ D radical substitution
◻ E condensation

What is meant by 'reaction mechanism'?

.................................................................................................................................

.................................................................................................................................

**10** The purpose of the ultraviolet radiation is:

◻ A to act as a catalyst
◻ B to heat up the reaction and make it go faster
◻ C to decompose the methane molecule
◻ D to prevent the reaction from going too fast
◻ E to provide energy to break the Br–Br bond

Write an equation to show a bromine molecule forming a bromine radical.

.................................................................................................................................

.................................................................................................................................

**11** During the reaction, Br• forms. Which of A–E correctly describes this particle? (Bromine is in group 7 of the periodic table.)

◻ A the outer shell electronic configuration of the particle is $ns^2$, $np^7$, where $n$ is the shell number
◻ B it is an ion
◻ C it is an atom with all electrons paired in orbitals
◻ D it has a complete outer shell of electrons
◻ E it is an atom with one unpaired electron

How many unpaired electrons are present on an oxygen atom (atomic number = 8) in its ground state?

.................................................................................................................................

.................................................................................................................................

Instructions for answering
questions 12–17:

A 1, 2 and 3 only are correct
B 1 and 3 only are correct
C 2 and 4 only are correct
D 4 only is correct
E some other response

**12** Correct statements about an alkane with the empirical formula $C_3H_7$ include:
(1) it is unsaturated
(2) it must be based on hexane and no other alkane
(3) it reacts quickly with bromine water
(4) if combusted in a limited supply of oxygen, carbon monoxide and water are possible products

   A      B      C      D      E

Write an equation to show the incomplete combustion of ethane.
..................................................................................................................................................
..................................................................................................................................................

**13** When decane vapour is cracked, ethene and an alkane are the major products. Correct statements about this reaction include:
(1) an aluminium oxide catalyst at 300°C would be a suitable condition
(2) a balanced chemical equation could be: $C_{10}H_{22}(g) \longrightarrow C_2H_4(g) + C_8H_{18}(g)$
(3) bromine water will be decolorised by the product mixture but not by the reactant
(4) one of the products of the reaction can be polymerised to form a polymer with this structure:

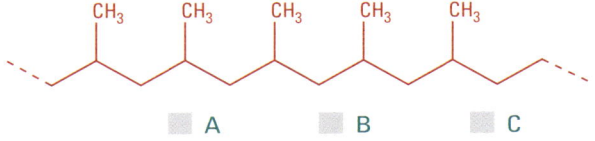

   A      B      C      D      E

Why is cracking of major importance in the petrochemical industry?
..................................................................................................................................................
..................................................................................................................................................
..................................................................................................................................................
..................................................................................................................................................

**14** When chlorine reacts with methane gas in the presence of ultraviolet light, likely propagation steps include:
(1) $Cl_2 + CH_3\bullet \longrightarrow CH_3Cl + Cl\bullet$
(2) $Cl_2 + CH_4 \longrightarrow CH_3Cl + HCl$
(3) $Cl_2 \longrightarrow 2Cl\bullet$
(4) $Cl\bullet + CH_4 \longrightarrow CH_3\bullet + HCl$

   A      B      C      D      E

What is meant by a propagation step?

....................................................................................................................................

....................................................................................................................................

**15** The graph shows relative molecular mass of the straight-chain alkanes (methane to decane) on the *x*-axis.
The quantity measured on the *y*-axis could be:
(1) boiling point
(2) flammability
(3) density
(4) viscosity

Relative molecular
mass of alkane

▨ A          ▨ B          ▨ C          ▨ D          ▨ E

Which is the more flammable, *n*-butane or 2-methylpropane? Explain your answer.

....................................................................................................................................

....................................................................................................................................

....................................................................................................................................

....................................................................................................................................

**16** Consider 1 dm$^3$ of methane gas and 1 dm$^3$ of propane gas measured under the same conditions of temperature and pressure. Correct statements about these two gases include:
(1) both samples of gas have the same mass
(2) when completely combusted, each gas reacts with the same volume of pure oxygen gas
(3) the gases can be easily distinguished by their differing reactions with bromine
(4) the gases have different densities

▨ A          ▨ B          ▨ C          ▨ D          ▨ E

When each volume of gas is ignited in excess oxygen, which of the two gases is expected to produce most heat energy?

....................................................................................................................................

....................................................................................................................................

**17** Correct statements about the alkane shown include:
(1) it is called methylcyclohexane
(2) it is a polar molecule
(3) molecules are attracted to each other by van der Waals forces
(4) it has a molecular formula of $C_7H_{13}$

CH$_3$

▨ A          ▨ B          ▨ C          ▨ D          ▨ E

What is the general formula of a typical cyclic alkane?

....................................................................................................................................

....................................................................................................................................

**18** Which of A–E correctly places the fractions from crude oil in order of increasing boiling point?

   A  petroleum gases; diesel oil; lubricating oil; fuel oil; gasoline; naphtha; kerosine; bitumen

   B  petroleum gases; gasoline; diesel oil; lubricating oil; naphtha; kerosine; fuel oil; bitumen

   C  petroleum gases; gasoline; naphtha; kerosine; diesel oil; lubricating oil; fuel oil; bitumen

   D  naphtha; kerosine; diesel oil; petroleum gases; gasoline; lubricating oil; fuel oil; bitumen

   E  gasoline; kerosine; diesel oil; petroleum gases; lubricating oil; naphtha; fuel oil; bitumen

What determines the magnitude of the van der Waals intermolecular forces acting between alkane molecules?

.................................................................................................................................................

.................................................................................................................................................

.................................................................................................................................................

# Alkenes

Questions 1 to 5 relate to the following formulae:

A $CH_3CH=CH_2$
B $H_2C=CH-CH=CH_2$
C $H_2C=CH(CH_2)_8CH_3$
D $H_2C=CH_2$
E $CH_3CH=CHCH_3$

**1** From the above, select an alkene capable of displaying geometric isomerism.

    A       B       C       D       E

Explain how a molecule is able to exist as geometric isomers.

.................................................................................................................................................

.................................................................................................................................................

.................................................................................................................................................

.................................................................................................................................................

**2** From the above, select the alkene missing from the equation:

$C_{10}H_{22}(g) \longrightarrow C_6H_{14}(g) + 2$................

    A       B       C       D       E

Write an equation to show the cracking of pentadecane vapour, $C_{15}H_{32}(g)$.

..................................................................................................................................................

..................................................................................................................................................

**3** From the above, select an alkene capable of reacting with excess hydrogen bromide to form only one organic product.

▢ A          ▢ B          ▢ C          ▢ D          ▢ E

Name the product formed in this reaction.

..................................................................................................................................................

..................................................................................................................................................

**4** From the above, select an alkene that, when polymerised, forms:

CH₃   CH₃   CH₃   CH₃   CH₃   CH₃

▢ A          ▢ B          ▢ C          ▢ D          ▢ E

Name this type of polymer.

..................................................................................................................................................

..................................................................................................................................................

**5** 1 mol of which alkene, A–E, will react with 2 mol of bromine, $Br_2$?

▢ A          ▢ B          ▢ C          ▢ D          ▢ E

Name the product of this reaction.

..................................................................................................................................................

..................................................................................................................................................

| Instructions for answering questions 6–11: | A 1, 2 and 3 only are correct<br>B 1 and 3 only are correct<br>C 2 and 4 only are correct<br>D 4 only is correct<br>E some other response |
|---|---|

**6** Correct statements about the mechanism of the reaction between ethene and bromine include:
(1) bromine acts as an electrophile
(2) the bromine molecule undergoes homolytic fission
(3) ethene donates an electron pair
(4) the reaction is a substitution

▢ A          ▢ B          ▢ C          ▢ D          ▢ E

What is meant by the term 'nucleophile' in an organic mechanism?

..................................................................................................................................................

..................................................................................................................................................

**7** Ethene reacts with bromine to form a new organic product. Correct statements about this reaction include:

(1) the molecular formula of the product is $C_2H_4Br_2$

(2) the product is colourless

(3) the reaction is known as an addition process

(4) the reaction takes place slowly

 A     B     C     D    E

What is meant by the term 'unsaturated'?

.............................................................................................................................................................................

.............................................................................................................................................................................

**8** When dodecane vapour, $C_{12}H_{26}(g)$, is cracked, ethene and another substance are formed. Correct statements about this process include:

(1) the other substance formed could be decane, $C_{10}H_{22}$

(2) the process requires oxygen

(3) the product mixture could decolorise bromine water

(4) aluminium oxide, at 300°C, can act as a catalyst for the process

A    B    C    D    E

Give a use for ethene. ..............................................................................................................................

.............................................................................................................................................................................

**9** A polymer has the following skeletal formula:

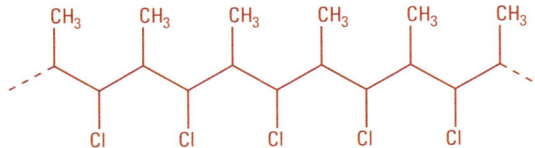

Correct statements about this polymer include:

(1) the polymer is unsaturated

(2) the monomer for synthesising the polymer could be:

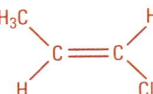

(3) the polymer is known as a condensation polymer

(4) the empirical formula for the polymer is $CH_2Cl$

A    B    C    D    E

What is the common name given to the polymer formed when tetrafluoroethene is polymerised?

.............................................................................................................................................................................

.............................................................................................................................................................................

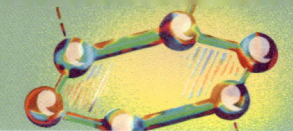

**10** An alkene is found to contain 87.8% carbon by mass. It is known to have a relative molecular mass of 82. (r.a.m. C = 12, H = 1)

Correct statements about the alkene include:

(1) it could have a straight-chain form

(2) its empirical formula is $CH_2$

(3) it could have a cyclic structure

(4) 1 mol of it could react with 2 mol of bromine molecules, $Br_2$

▧ A      ▧ B      ▧ C      ▧ D      ▧ E

Show your working.

........................................................................................................................................................

........................................................................................................................................................

........................................................................................................................................................

........................................................................................................................................................

**11** Correct statements about the molecule shown include:

(1) it is saturated

(2) it will not react with bromine water

(3) it is non-polar

(4) it should polymerise to form an addition polymer

▧ A      ▧ B      ▧ C      ▧ D      ▧ E

What is the molecular formula of the molecule featured in this question?

........................................................................................................................................................

........................................................................................................................................................

**12** How many electrons are there in a carbon–carbon double bond?

▧ A 1

▧ B 2

▧ C 3

▧ D 4

▧ E 6

Name the two molecular orbitals that constitute a typical C=C bond.

........................................................................................................................................................

........................................................................................................................................................

**13** In the following sequence, the values of which of the properties A–E *decrease* in the order shown?

$C_2H_4$, $C_3H_6$, $C_4H_8$, $C_5H_{10}$, $C_6H_{12}$

▧ A molecular mass

▧ B viscosity

▧ C flammability

▧ D the amount of bromine with which 1 mol of each reacts

▧ E solubility in a polar solvent

Using equimolar quantities, which of the alkenes in this sequence would react with oxygen most exothermically?

........................................................................................

........................................................................................

Questions 14–18 refer to the following organic synthesis:

Cyclohexene may be prepared in the laboratory by warming exactly 5.00 g of cyclohexanol with excess concentrated phosphoric(V) acid under reflux. The equation for the reaction is:

OH

$\xrightarrow{H_3PO_4}$

+ $H_2O$

(r.a.m. C = 12, H = 1, O = 16)

**14** Reflux means:

   A heating the reactants strongly
   B the process of converting a liquid into a solid
   C the removal of water from a substance
   D the continual processes of evaporation and condensation
   E removal of the product as soon as it is formed

Why could reflux be of use in an organic reaction?

........................................................................................

........................................................................................

**15** Which of A–E best describes the role of phosphoric(V) acid in the reaction?

   A reducing agent
   B dehydrating agent
   C oxidising agent
   D an impurity to lower the boiling point of the product
   E an immiscible solvent that selectively dissolves the product

Write an equation, using molecular formulae, to describe this reaction.

........................................................................................

........................................................................................

**16** In the first stage of separation of the cyclohexene, an organic solvent is added to the product mixture. The solvent is added because:

   A it dissolves the impurities selectively
   B it causes the product to form a gas, which can be collected easily
   C it reacts with the reactants and impurities
   D it causes the product to crystallise
   E it dissolves the cyclohexene and any other non-polar compounds selectively

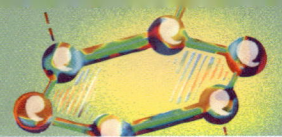

Having carried out the above process, how would the product then be separated?

...........................................................................................................................................................

...........................................................................................................................................................

...........................................................................................................................................................

...........................................................................................................................................................

**17** In a synthesis, 2.45 g of
cyclohexene is formed. The
percentage yield of product is:

☐ A 2.45%
☐ B 2.45 × (100/82)%
☐ C (5.00 × 100/82)%
☐ D 59.8%
☐ E (5.00 × 82/100)%

Show your working.

...........................................................................................................................................................

...........................................................................................................................................................

...........................................................................................................................................................

...........................................................................................................................................................

**18** Under certain conditions, the product of the reaction can be polymerised. The correct repeat unit
for the product of this polymerisation is:

☐ A

☐ B

☐ C

☐ D

☐ E

Name this type of polymer.

...........................................................................................................................................................

...........................................................................................................................................................

# Halogenoalkanes

Questions 1–6 refer to the
following compounds:

A $CH_3CH(Br)CH_3$
B $C_2H_5Cl$
C $CF_4$
D $C_2H_5Br$
E $CH_3(CH_2)_2Br$

**1** Which of A–E does not possess an overall dipole moment?

▨ A ▨ B ▨ C ▨ D ▨ E

What is meant by 'a bond possesses a dipole'?

..........................................................................................................................................

..........................................................................................................................................

**2** Which of A–E will form a white precipitate when treated with silver(I) nitrate solution and warmed?

▨ A ▨ B ▨ C ▨ D ▨ E

Write an ionic equation to show how the precipitate in this question is formed.

..........................................................................................................................................

..........................................................................................................................................

**3** Which of A–E is a secondary halogenalkane?

▨ A ▨ B ▨ C ▨ D ▨ E

Is 2-bromo-2-methylpropane a primary, secondary or tertiary halogenoalkane?

..........................................................................................................................................

..........................................................................................................................................

**4** Which of A–E will form a precipitate with hot, aqueous silver(I) nitrate least rapidly?

▨ A ▨ B ▨ C ▨ D ▨ E

What determines the rate at which the precipitate will form?

..........................................................................................................................................

..........................................................................................................................................

**5** Which of A–E will form ethanol and a cream precipitate when treated with aqueous silver(I) nitrate and heated?

▨ A ▨ B ▨ C ▨ D ▨ E

What is the name of the mechanism for this reaction?

..........................................................................................................................................

..........................................................................................................................................

**6** Which of A–E will react with ethanolic ammonia to form:

$$H_3C \diagdown \diagup CH_2$$
$$CH_2 \diagup \diagdown NH_2$$

▨ A ▨ B ▨ C ▨ D ▨ E

To which class of organic compounds does the product of this reaction belong?

..........................................................................................................................................

..........................................................................................................................................

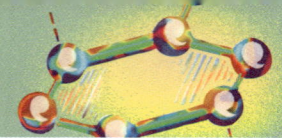

**7** Which of statements A–E about this halogenoalkane is correct?

- A it has a molecular formula of $C_6H_{10}Cl$
- B it is non-polar
- C it is called chlorobenzene
- D it will react with aqueous sodium hydroxide solution, under reflux, to form $C_6H_{11}OH$
- E it will form a yellow precipitate when treated with warm silver(I) nitrate solution

Starting with cyclohexanol, how could this molecule be synthesised?

.....................................................................................................................................................................

.....................................................................................................................................................................

Questions 8–11 are concerned with the following reaction scheme:

$$H-\overset{\overset{\displaystyle H}{|}}{\underset{\underset{\displaystyle H}{|}}{C}}-\overset{\overset{\displaystyle H}{|}}{\underset{\underset{\displaystyle H}{|}}{C}}-H \longrightarrow H-\overset{\overset{\displaystyle H}{|}}{\underset{\underset{\displaystyle H}{|}}{C}}-\overset{\overset{\displaystyle H}{|}}{\underset{\underset{\displaystyle H}{|}}{C}}-Br \longrightarrow H-\overset{\overset{\displaystyle H}{|}}{\underset{\underset{\displaystyle H}{|}}{C}}-\overset{\overset{\displaystyle H}{|}}{\underset{\underset{\displaystyle H}{|}}{C}}-NH_2$$

X                              Y                              Z

**8** The name of the mechanism taking place when X is converted to Y is:

- A nucleophilic substitution
- B electrophilic addition
- C nucleophilic addition
- D radical substitution
- E electrophilic substitution

What is an electrophile?

.....................................................................................................................................................................

.....................................................................................................................................................................

**9** The reagents and conditions required to convert X into Y are:

- A hydrogen bromide; room temperature and pressure
- B bromine; ultraviolet light
- C hydrogen bromide; ultraviolet light
- D sodium bromide solution; heat under reflux
- E bromine water; room temperature and pressure

Why do some organic reactions need to be heated?

.....................................................................................................................................................................

.....................................................................................................................................................................

**10** The optimum reagents and conditions for the conversion of Y into Z are:

- A concentrated nitric acid, $HNO_3$; heat under reflux
- B ammonia in ethanol; heat under reflux
- C aqueous ammonia; room temperature and pressure
- D ammonia; ultraviolet light
- E nitrogen gas; under pressure

What is the name of molecule Y?

..................................................................................................................................

..................................................................................................................................

**11** What is the name of the
mechanism taking place when Y
is converted to Z?

    A radical substitution
    B electrophilic addition
    C electrophilic substitution
    D nucleophilic substitution
    E nucleophilic addition

What is the name of molecule Z?

..................................................................................................................................

..................................................................................................................................

**12** When this substance is treated with pure ethanol in which potassium hydroxide has been
dissolved, and heated, which of products A–E could form?

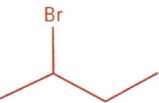

    A only butan-2-ol
    B only but-1-ene
    C 2,3-dibromobutane
    D a mixture of butan-1-ol and butan-2-ol
    E a mixture of but-1-ene and but-2-ene

What is the purpose of the ethanol in the reaction?

..................................................................................................................................

..................................................................................................................................

Questions 13–16 are concerned with the following general mechanism:

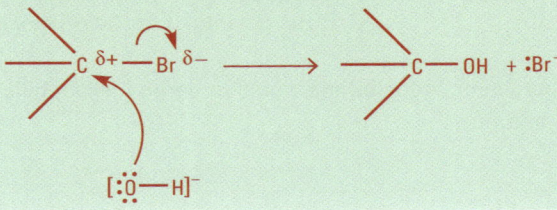

**13** In which of reactions A–E is this
mechanism relevant?

    A $C_2H_4$ and $Br_2$
    B $CH_4$ and $Br_2$ in the presence of ultraviolet radiation
    C NaOH (ethanol) and $C_5H_{11}Br$
    D KOH(aq) and $C_3H_7Br$
    E $C_2H_4$ and HBr

What is the name of the nucleophile in the mechanism shown?

..................................................................................................................................

..................................................................................................................................

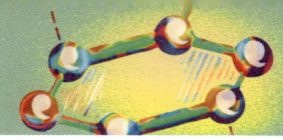

**14** In the reaction, the hydroxide ion acts as:

- A a radical
- B a proton donor
- C an electrophile
- D a catalyst
- E a nucleophile

Why does the hydroxide ion attack the carbon atom in the halogenoalkane?

.................................................................................................................................................................

.................................................................................................................................................................

.................................................................................................................................................................

.................................................................................................................................................................

**15** Which of A–E occurs to the C–Br bond in the mechanism?

- A it is oxidised
- B homolytic fission
- C the carbon atom is attacked by an electrophile
- D heterolytic fission
- E both electrons in the C–Br bond move to the carbon atom

What is meant by the term 'homolytic fission'?

.................................................................................................................................................................

.................................................................................................................................................................

**16** The reactivity of the halogenoalkane in the mechanism is determined by:

- A the magnitude of the intermolecular forces between the halogenoalkane molecules
- B the strength of the carbon–halogen bond
- C the relative molecular mass of the halogenoalkane
- D the rate at which the molecule can diffuse in solution
- E the polarity of the halogenoalkane

Which of 1-chlorobutane or 1-iodobutane would undergo nucleophilic substitution at the faster rate? Explain your answer.

.................................................................................................................................................................

.................................................................................................................................................................

Questions 17–18 are concerned with the following reaction mechanism which takes place using ethanolic potassium hydroxide:

$$\begin{array}{cc} H & H \\ | & | \\ H-C-C-Br \\ | & | \\ H & H \end{array}$$

$[H-\ddot{O}:]^{-}$

**17** Which of A–E best describes the role of the hydroxide ion in the reaction?

    A a nucleophile
    B a radical
    C a base
    D an electrophile
    E a catalyst

What is the meaning of a curly arrow in a mechanism?

..................................................................................................................................

..................................................................................................................................

**18** The expected products from this reaction are:

    A $C_2H_4$, $H_2O$ and $Br^-$
    B $C_2H_5OH$ and $Br^-$
    C $C_2H_4$ and HBr
    D $C_2H_5OH$ and HBr
    E $CH_3CH_2Br$ and $H_2O$

Write a chemical equation for this reaction.

..................................................................................................................................

..................................................................................................................................

# Alcohols

Instructions for answering questions 1–5:

A 1, 2 and 3 only are correct
B 1 and 3 only are correct
C 2 and 4 only are correct
D 4 only is correct
E some other response

Questions 1–5 concern the following compounds:

(1) $CH_3CH_2CH(OH)CH_3$
(2) $C_2H_5OH$
(3) $CH_3CH(OH)CH_3$
(4) $CH_3C(CH_3)(OH)CH_3$

**1** Which of the above is/are secondary alcohols?

    A      B      C      D      E

To which class of alcohol does cyclohexanol belong?

..................................................................................................................................

..................................................................................................................................

**2** Which of the above will not be oxidised on heating with acidified potassium dichromate(VI)?

    A      B      C      D      E

Explain why the compound you have identified is not oxidised under normal conditions.

..................................................................................................................................

..................................................................................................................................

..................................................................................................................................

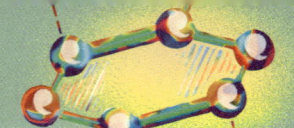

**3** Which of the above exist(s) as optical isomers?

◼ A          ◼ B          ◼ C          ◼ D          ◼ E

What criteria need to be satisfied for a molecule to exist as optical isomers?

..............................................................................................................................................

..............................................................................................................................................

..............................................................................................................................................

**4** Which of the above will react with methanoic acid, HCOOH, in the presence of concentrated sulphuric acid, to form:

```
           CH₃
      H     |     H
      |     |     |
 H — C  —  C  —  C — H
      |     |     |
      H     |     H
            O     O
             \   //
              C
              |
              H
```

◼ A          ◼ B          ◼ C          ◼ D          ◼ E

Name the compound with the structural formula $CH_3CH_2CH_2OCOCH_3$.

..............................................................................................................................................

..............................................................................................................................................

**5** Which of the above will form ethene when heated with concentrated sulphuric acid?

◼ A          ◼ B          ◼ C          ◼ D          ◼ E

What is the chemical role of the concentrated sulphuric acid in this reaction?

..............................................................................................................................................

..............................................................................................................................................

**6** This compound is called:

```
      H     H    OH    H
      |     |     |    |
 H — C  —  C  —  C  — C — H
      |     |     |    |
      H     H     |    H
                 C₂H₅
```

◼ A 2-ethylbutan-2-ol
◼ B butan-2-ol
◼ C 3-hydroxy-3-methylpentane
◼ D ethylbutan-2-ol
◼ E 3-methylpentan-3-ol

To which class of alcohols does this compound belong?

..............................................................................................................................................

..............................................................................................................................................

**7**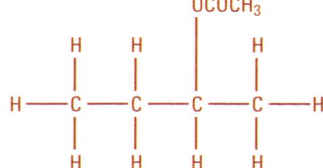

This ester can be synthesised from the following pairs of substances:

A butan-1-ol and methanoic acid
B butan-2-ol and ethanoic acid
C methanol and pentanoic acid
D butan-1-ol and ethanoic acid
E butanoic acid and ethanol

Name a catalyst that would be appropriate in a reaction of this type.

**8** Sodium bromide and concentrated sulphuric acid are added to propan-2-ol and the mixture is heated under reflux. The molecule that forms in the greatest yield is:

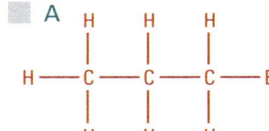

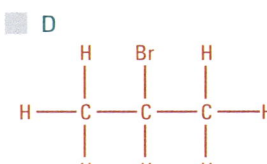

Sodium bromide and concentrated sulphuric acid produce an intermediate in this reaction, which then reacts with the alcohol. Name the intermediate.

**9** When butan-2-ol is heated with concentrated sulphuric acid, how many different structural isomers that are alkenes could be formed?

A 5
B 4
C 3
D 2
E 1

Can any of the alkenes formed in this reaction exist as geometric isomers? Explain your answer.

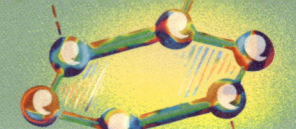

**10** The correct structure of the product formed when sodium is added to ethanol is:

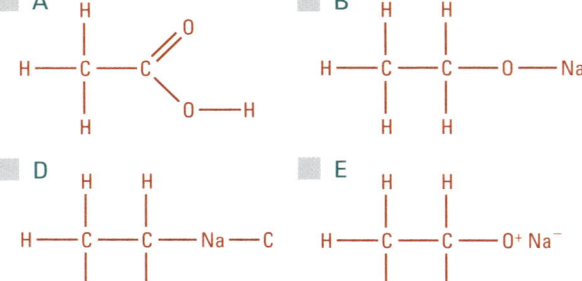

How does the alcohol behave on reacting with sodium?

**11** Ethanol may be oxidised to form ethanal and then ethanoic acid. The correct formulae of ethanal and ethanoic acid respectively are:

A $CH_3CH_2OH$ and $CH_3CH_2OCOCH_3$
B $C_2H_4$ and $CH_3CH_2OH$
C $CH_3CHO$ and $CH_3COOH$
D $CH_3COOH$ and $CH_2(OH)CH_2(OH)$
E $C_2H_5OH$ and $CH_3CHO$

Give the name and formula of the straight-chain carboxylic acid containing five carbon atoms.

Instructions for answering questions 12–17:

A 1, 2 and 3 only are correct
B 1 and 3 only are correct
C 2 and 4 only are correct
D 4 only is correct
E some other response

**12** True statements about this compound include:
(1) it reacts with sodium to yield hydrogen gas
(2) it decolorises bromine water
(3) 1 mol of the compound reacts with 2 mol of HBr
(4) under normal conditions it can be oxidised to form a carboxylic acid

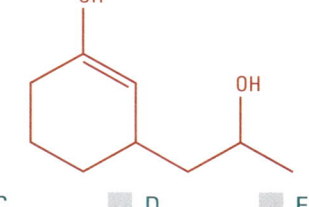

◼ A    ◼ B    ◼ C    ◼ D    ◼ E

On heating with concentrated sulphuric acid, will this compound be dehydrated?

**13** True statements about the reaction between methanol, $CH_3OH$, and sodium include:

(1) sodium is reduced

(2) methanol behaves as an acid

(3) methanol behaves as a nucleophile

(4) $CH_3O^-Na^+$ and $H_2$ form

    ▨ A       ▨ B       ▨ C       ▨ D       ▨ E

Write a chemical equation for this reaction.

.................................................................................................................................

.................................................................................................................................

**14** Propan-1-ol and propan-2-ol dissolve in each other in all proportions.

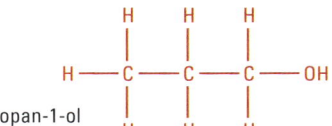 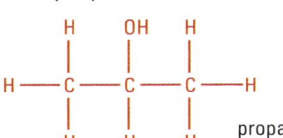

The intermolecular interactions that take place between these molecules are:

(1) dipole–dipole

(2) hydrogen bonding

(3) van der Waals

(4) ion–dipole

    ▨ A       ▨ B       ▨ C       ▨ D       ▨ E

Name the dominant intermolecular force acting between ethanal molecules.

.................................................................................................................................

.................................................................................................................................

**15** The colour change observed when ethanol is heated with acidified potassium dichromate(VI) is:

   ▨ A yellow to red

   ▨ B white to blue

   ▨ C red to blue

   ▨ D blue to brown

   ▨ E orange to green

How does the oxidation number of chromium change in this reaction?

.................................................................................................................................

.................................................................................................................................

**16** True statements about the reaction that takes place when methanol is refluxed with acidified potassium dichromate(VI) include:

(1) a relevant equation is $CH_3OH \longrightarrow HCHO + 2H^+ + 2e^-$

(2) acid catalyses the reaction

(3) carbon dioxide could form

(4) the dichromate(VI) ion is oxidised

    ▨ A       ▨ B       ▨ C       ▨ D       ▨ E

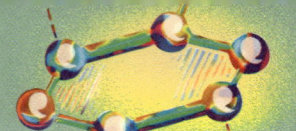

Write a half-equation to show what happens to the dichromate(VI) ion in the reaction.

**17** Relevant reasons explaining why alcohols are polar molecules include:
(1) all atoms are non-metallic elements
(2) all atoms have similar electronegativity
(3) hydrogen and carbon differ considerably in their electronegativity
(4) oxygen and hydrogen differ considerably in their electronegativity

    A        B        C        D        E

Why do most alcohols dissolve in water?

**18** When ethanol is added to a strong acid, the following process occurs:

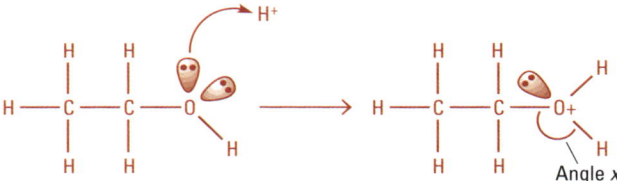

Correct statements about this process include:
(1) the value of angle *x* is approximately 120°
(2) the oxygen atom forms a dative bond with a proton
(3) ethanol behaves as an acid in this reaction
(4) the curly arrow originates from a lone pair of electrons

    A        B        C        D        E

Give another name for a hydrogen ion.

# General questions

| Questions 1–6 are concerned with the following numerical responses: | A 0 |
| --- | --- |
| | B 1 |
| | C 2 |
| | D 3 |
| | E 4 |

**1** The maximum number of structural isomers possible for the molecular formula $C_3H_6Cl_2$ is:

▨ A          ▨ B          ▨ C          ▨ D          ▨ E

What are they?

.................................................................................................................................................................

.................................................................................................................................................................

**2** The number of geometric isomers possible for $C_4H_8$ is:

▨ A          ▨ B          ▨ C          ▨ D          ▨ E

How many structural isomers (all alkenes) are possible for a molecule having the molecular formula $C_4H_8$?

.................................................................................................................................................................

.................................................................................................................................................................

**3** The number of optical isomers possible for a compound with two chiral carbon atoms per molecule is:

▨ A          ▨ B          ▨ C          ▨ D          ▨ E

Is butan-2-ol chiral? Explain your answer.

.................................................................................................................................................................

.................................................................................................................................................................

**4** The number of different groups attached to a carbon atom in a chiral molecule is:

▨ A          ▨ B          ▨ C          ▨ D          ▨ E

Is the molecule that has the structural formula $CH_3CH(OH)CN$ chiral? Explain your answer.

.................................................................................................................................................................

.................................................................................................................................................................

**5** The number of electrons present in a pi-bond in a molecule of ethane is:

▨ A          ▨ B          ▨ C          ▨ D          ▨ E

Which two molecular orbitals comprise a C=C bond in an alkene?

.................................................................................................................................................................

.................................................................................................................................................................

**6** The number of bonded pairs of electrons present in the species $CH_3^+$ is:

▨ A          ▨ B          ▨ C          ▨ D          ▨ E

What three-dimensional shape is expected for the $CH_3^+$ ion? Explain your answer.

.................................................................................................................................................................

.................................................................................................................................................................

.................................................................................................................................................................

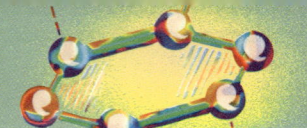

Questions 7–10 are concerned with the following reaction scheme:

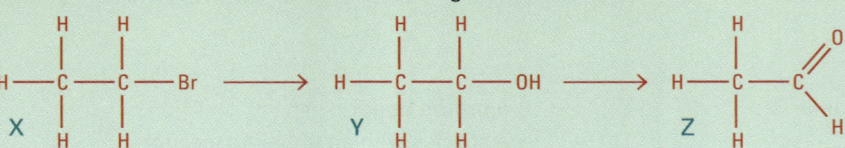

**7** The mechanism by which compound X is converted to compound Y is called:

    A nucleophilic substitution
    B radical substitution
    C nucleophilic addition
    D electrophilic addition
    E electrophilic substitution

To which organic family does molecule X belong?

.................................................................................................................................................

.................................................................................................................................................

**8** The reagents and conditions needed to convert X into Y are:

    A $K_2Cr_2O_7(aq)$ and dilute $H_2SO_4(aq)$; heat under reflux
    B KOH in ethanol; heat
    C $NH_3$ in ethanol; heat
    D $H_2$ gas; nickel catalyst at 150°C
    E NaOH(aq); heat under reflux

Which compound, X or Y, should be more soluble in water? Explain your answer.

.................................................................................................................................................

.................................................................................................................................................

**9** The following half-equation describes what happens to ethanol in the conversion of Y into Z:

$$C_2H_5OH \longrightarrow CH_3CHO + 2H^+ + 2e^-$$

Given this information, it can be deduced that:

    A ethanol has been reduced
    B the average oxidation number of carbon in ethanol has increased
    C ethanol is an oxidising agent
    D this is not a redox process
    E ethanol is behaving as a catalyst

What is the average oxidation number of carbon in $C_2H_5OH$ and $CH_3CHO$?

.................................................................................................................................................

.................................................................................................................................................

**10** The conversion of Y into Z is:

    A an oxidation
    B an addition reaction
    C a substitution reaction
    D polymerisation
    E neutralisation

Name compound Z.

.....................................................................................

.....................................................................................

**11** A nucleophile is:

      A a proton donor

      B a species with an unpaired electron

      C an electron pair donor

      D an electron-deficient species

      E always a negatively charged ion

Is a water molecule expected to be a nucleophile? Explain your answer.

.....................................................................................

.....................................................................................

**12** Which of A–E is a propagation process in the reaction between methane and bromine gas, in a 1:1 stoichiometric ratio, in the presence of ultraviolet light?

      A $Br_2 + CH_4 \longrightarrow CH_3Br + HBr$

      B $Br_2 \longrightarrow 2Br\bullet$

      C $Br\bullet + CH_4 \longrightarrow CH_3\bullet + HBr$

      D $Br_2 + CH_4 \longrightarrow CH_2Br_2 + 2HBr$

      E $Br\bullet + CH_4 \longrightarrow CH_3Br + H\bullet$

What further propagation steps are expected if the product of the reaction ($CH_3Br$) reacts with more bromine to form $CH_2Br_2$?

.....................................................................................

.....................................................................................

**13** When this substance is heated with ethanolic potassium hydroxide, which of A–E would be formed with the greatest yield?

  A 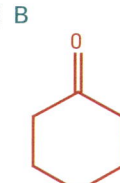      B       C       D      E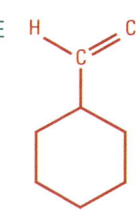

What type of reaction is occurring?

.....................................................................................

.....................................................................................

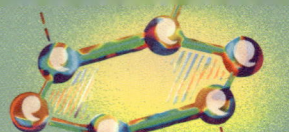

**14** This compound is called:

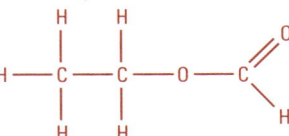

- A ethyl ethanoate
- B ethyl methanal
- C ethoxymethane
- D propanoic acid
- E ethyl methanoate

To which class of compounds does it belong?

..................................................................................................................................................................

..................................................................................................................................................................

Questions 15–17 refer to the conversion of bromoethane into ethylamine:

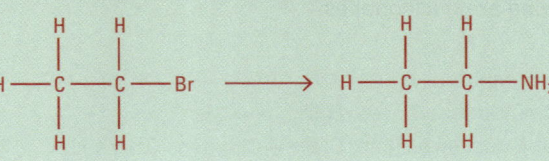

**15** The mechanism of this conversion is called:

- A nucleophilic substitution
- B redox
- C electrophilic substitution
- D nucleophilic addition
- E radical substitution

Give the formula of the nucleophile in the reaction.

..................................................................................................................................................................

..................................................................................................................................................................

**16** The reagents and conditions required for this conversion are:

- A methylamine, $CH_3NH_2$; heat
- B concentrated nitric acid; room temperature and pressure
- C ammonia in ethanol; heat under reflux
- D ethanolic KOH; reflux
- E nitrogen gas; 450°C

Suggest how the product of the reaction may react with dilute hydrochloric acid. (Hint — how does ammonia react with acid?)

..................................................................................................................................................................

..................................................................................................................................................................

**17** Exactly 3.50 g of bromoethane was used in an experiment and it was found that at the end of the reaction 0.82 g of ethylamine had formed. The approximate percentage yield of product in this reaction was:
(r.a.m. C = 12, H = 1, O = 16, N = 14, Br = 80)

- A 10%
- B 15%
- C 57%
- D 23%
- E 1.5%

Show your working.

.....................................................................................................................................................

.....................................................................................................................................................

| Instructions for answering question 18: | A 1, 2 and 3 only are correct |
|---|---|
| | B 1 and 3 only are correct |
| | C 2 and 4 only are correct |
| | D 4 only is correct |
| | E some other response |

**18** Which of the following are nucleophiles?

(1) $OH^-$

(2) $H^+$

(3) $NH_3$

(4) $K^+$

      A       B       C       D       E

What essential structural feature must a nucleophile possess?

.....................................................................................................................................................

.....................................................................................................................................................

# Physical chemistry

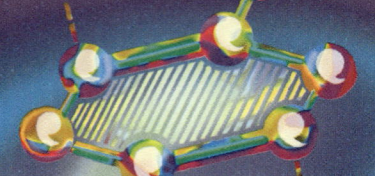

## Enthalpy changes

| Questions 1–5 are concerned with the following chemical changes: | A $Ca(s) + Cl_2(g) \longrightarrow CaCl_2(s)$<br>B $Na(g) \longrightarrow Na^+(g) + e^-$<br>C $\frac{1}{2}Cl_2(g) \longrightarrow Cl(g)$<br>D $CH_3OH(l) + \frac{3}{2}O_2(g) \longrightarrow CO_2(g) + 2H_2O(l)$<br>E $NaOH(aq) + HCl(aq) \longrightarrow NaCl(aq) + H_2O(l)$ |
|---|---|

**1** A reaction that represents an enthalpy of combustion is:

       ■ A        ■ B        ■ C        ■ D        ■ E

Write an equation to show the enthalpy of combustion of sulphur.

......................................................................................................................................

......................................................................................................................................

**2** A reaction that represents an enthalpy of atomisation is:

       ■ A        ■ B        ■ C        ■ D        ■ E

Write an equation to show the enthalpy of atomisation of carbon.

......................................................................................................................................

......................................................................................................................................

**3** A reaction that represents an enthalpy of formation is:

       ■ A        ■ B        ■ C        ■ D        ■ E

Write an equation to show the enthalpy of formation of sodium carbonate.

......................................................................................................................................

......................................................................................................................................

**4** A reaction that represents ionisation energy is:

       ■ A        ■ B        ■ C        ■ D        ■ E

Write an equation to show the second ionisation energy of aluminium.

......................................................................................................................................

......................................................................................................................................

**5** A reaction that represents an enthalpy of neutralisation is:

       ■ A        ■ B        ■ C        ■ D        ■ E

Write an ionic equation for the reaction chosen.

......................................................................................................................................

......................................................................................................................................

**6** The following reaction is exothermic and produces 11 kJ mol$^{-1}$:

$I_2(g) + Cl_2(g) \longrightarrow 2ICl(g)$

(Bond energy/kJ mol$^{-1}$: I–I = 151; Cl–Cl = 242)
Using these figures, what is the value (in kJ mol$^{-1}$) for
the bond energy of I–Cl?

- A 202
- B 393
- C 191
- D 382
- E 404

Show your working.

..........

**7** Consider the reaction:

$2Na(s) + 2H_2O(l) \longrightarrow 2NaOH(s) + H_2(g)$

($\Delta H_f$ /kJ mol$^{-1}$: $H_2O(l)$ = –285.9; NaOH(s) = –427)
What is the enthalpy change (in kJ) associated with this
reaction?

- A –1425.8
- B –282.2
- C –712.9
- D –141.1
- E +712.9

Show your working.

..........

**8** Consider the following general energy cycle:

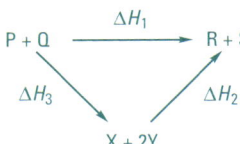

Given that $\Delta H_1$ = –150 kJ mol$^{-1}$ and $\Delta H_2$ = –50 kJ mol$^{-1}$,
what is the value for $\Delta H_3$?

- A +100
- B +50
- C +200
- D –100
- E –200

Show your working.

..........

**9** The standard enthalpy of formation of
calcium carbonate relates to the equation:

- A $CaCO_3(s) \longrightarrow CaO(s) + CO_2(s)$
- B $Ca(s) + C(g) + \frac{3}{2}O_2(g) \longrightarrow CaCO_3(s)$
- C $Ca(s) + C(s) + \frac{3}{2}O_2(g) \longrightarrow CaCO_3(s)$
- D $Ca^{2+}(g) + C^{4+}(g) + 3O^{2-}(g) \longrightarrow CaCO_3(s)$
- E $2Ca(s) + 2C(s) + 3O_2(g) \longrightarrow 2\,CaCO_3(s)$

Define standard enthalpy of formation.

..........

**10** Consider the reaction:

$$2CO(g) + O_2(g) \longrightarrow 2CO_2(g)$$

(Bond energy data/kJ mol$^{-1}$: O=O = 496;

C=O = 743; C$\equiv$O = 1053)

Using the average bond energies given, what is the enthalpy change associated with this reaction?

A −806

B +370

C −620

D +806

E −370

Show your working.

| Instructions for answering questions 11–16: | A 1, 2 and 3 only are correct |
| --- | --- |
| | B 1 and 3 only are correct |
| | C 2 and 4 only are correct |
| | D 4 only is correct |
| | E some other response |

**11** Hexane is combusted according to the following equation:

$$C_6H_{14}(l) + \tfrac{19}{2}O_2(g) \longrightarrow 6CO_2(g) + 7H_2O(l) \quad \Delta H = -4194 \text{ kJ mol}^{-1}$$

(r.a.m. C = 12, H = 1)

True statements about this reaction include:

(1) 4194 kJ of heat energy are absorbed per mole of hexane

(2) approximately 49 kJ of heat energy are released per gram of hexane

(3) 4194 kJ is the activation energy for the reaction

(4) more heat energy is evolved on forming new bonds in the products than heat energy absorbed when breaking bonds in the reactants

A        B        C        D        E

Define enthalpy change.

**12** The standard enthalpy changes of formation of graphite and diamond are 0 and +1.2 kJ mol$^{-1}$ respectively. Given this information, true statements include:

(1) diamond is the more thermodynamically stable form of carbon

(2) the enthalpy change associated with the reaction C(graphite) $\longrightarrow$ C(diamond) is −1.2 kJ mol$^{-1}$

(3) the conversion from graphite to diamond is fast

(4) graphite is more thermodynamically stable than diamond, by 1.2 kJ mol$^{-1}$

A        B        C        D        E

When both forms of carbon are combusted, which form produces more heat energy?

**13** Enthalpy changes measured specifically in the gas phase are:
 (1) ionisation energy
 (2) enthalpy of combustion
 (3) bond energy
 (4) enthalpy of formation

     A       B       C       D       E

Write an equation that shows the average bond energy of the C–H bond in methane.

........................................................................................................................

........................................................................................................................

**14** Which of the following would have a negative $\Delta H$ value?
 (1) $CuSO_4(s) + 5H_2O(l) \longrightarrow CuSO_4.5H_2O(s)$
 (2) $CH_4(g) + 2O_2(g) \longrightarrow CO_2(g) + 2H_2O(l)$
 (3) $Mg^+(g) + e^- \longrightarrow Mg(g)$
 (4) $F_2(g) \longrightarrow 2F(g)$

     A       B       C       D       E

Consider the following reactions:
 $Cl_2(g) \longrightarrow 2Cl(g)$
 $I_2(g) \longrightarrow 2I(g)$

Which is the more endothermic?

........................................................................................................................

........................................................................................................................

**15** When $10\,cm^3$ of $2.0\,mol\,dm^{-3}$ sodium hydroxide solution was added to $10\,cm^3$ of $2.0\,mol\,dm^{-3}$ sulphuric acid, a temperature rise of 14°C was observed.
 The equation for the reaction is $2NaOH(aq) + H_2SO_4(aq) \longrightarrow Na_2SO_4(aq) + 2H_2O(l)$.
 The specific heat capacity of water is $4.2\,J\,K^{-1}\,g^{-1}$.

Given this information, true statements include:
 (1) $5.0\,cm^3$ of the original sodium hydroxide solution is unused
 (2) approximately 1175 J of heat energy is evolved in the reaction
 (3) the reaction absorbs heat energy from the surroundings
 (4) $\Delta H$ is approximately $-58.8\,kJ\,mol^{-1}$

     A       B       C       D       E

How would the enthalpy change for the following reaction be expected to differ from that of the previous reaction? Explain your answer.
 $KOH(aq) + HCl(aq) \longrightarrow KCl(aq) + H_2O(l)$

........................................................................................................................

........................................................................................................................

........................................................................................................................

........................................................................................................................

**16** The enthalpy of formation of ammonium chloride, $NH_4Cl(s)$, is $-315\,kJ\,mol^{-1}$. Given this information, it can be deduced that ammonium chloride:

(1) is less thermodynamically stable than its constituent elements, by $315\,kJ\,mol^{-1}$

(2) often reacts with a high activation energy

(3) is soluble in water

(4) is more stable than its constituent elements, by $315\,kJ\,mol^{-1}$

        ▨ A        ▨ B        ▨ C        ▨ D        ▨ E

Write an equation to show ammonium chloride dissolving in water.

..........................................................................................................................................................

..........................................................................................................................................................

**17** Consider the following energy cycle:

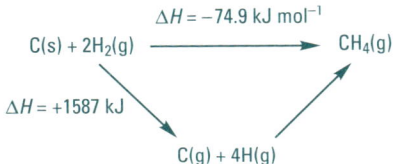

Using this information, the value for the average bond energy (in $kJ\,mol^{-1}$) of the C–H bond in methane is approximately:

▨ A  $-415$
▨ B  $+1662$
▨ C  $+1512$
▨ D  $+378$
▨ E  $+415$

Show your working.

..........................................................................................................................................................

..........................................................................................................................................................

**18** Consider the following reaction:

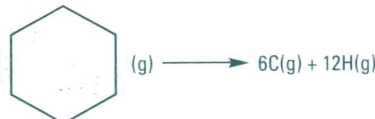

The correct value for the enthalpy change (in $kJ\,mol^{-1}$) associated with this reaction is:

(Bond energy/$kJ\,mol^{-1}$: C–C = 348; C–H = 412)

▨ A  $-7032$
▨ B  $-760$
▨ C  $+64$
▨ D  $+1172$
▨ E  $+7032$

Show your working.

..........................................................................................................................................................

..........................................................................................................................................................

# Rates of reaction

Questions 1–5 are concerned with the following five graphical variations:

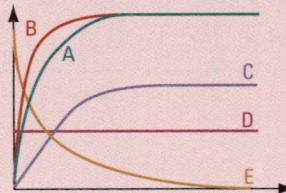

**1** The graph that best describes the mass of a catalyst with time during a reaction is:

          A         B        C        D        E

What is a catalyst?

............................................................................................................................................

............................................................................................................................................

............................................................................................................................................

............................................................................................................................................

**2** Select the graph that best describes the mass of magnesium carbonate remaining with time, in the reaction:

$$MgCO_3(s) + 2HCl(aq) \longrightarrow MgCl_2(aq) + H_2O(l) + CO_2(g)$$

          A         B        C        D        E

Suggest one other way in which the rate of this reaction could be followed.

............................................................................................................................................

............................................................................................................................................

............................................................................................................................................

............................................................................................................................................

Questions 3–5 are also concerned with the following experiment:
5.00 g of magnesium ribbon (an excess) is placed in each of three separate solutions of dilute hydrochloric acid. The volume of hydrogen produced is collected and measured with time.

**3** The graph that represents the use of 100 cm$^3$ of 2.0 mol dm$^{-3}$ hydrochloric acid at 20°C is:

          A         B        C        D        E

How many moles of hydrochloric acid are present in 100 cm$^3$ of concentration 2.0 mol dm$^{-3}$?

............................................................................................................................................

............................................................................................................................................

**4** The graph that represents the use of 100 cm$^3$ of 2.0 mol dm$^{-3}$ hydrochloric acid at 40°C is:

          A         B        C        D        E

How is the rate of a chemical reaction affected by an increase in temperature?

............................................................................................................................................

............................................................................................................................................

............................................................................................................................................

**5** The graph that represents the use of 50 cm$^3$ of 2.0 mol dm$^{-3}$ hydrochloric acid and 50.0 cm$^3$ of water at 20°C is:

▨ A      ▨ B      ▨ C      ▨ D      ▨ E

Comment on the total amount of gas produced in this case, compared with the volumes produced in questions 3 and 4.

...................................................................................................................................................

...................................................................................................................................................

...................................................................................................................................................

...................................................................................................................................................

| Instructions for answering questions 6–11: | A 1, 2 and 3 only are correct<br>B 1 and 3 only are correct<br>C 2 and 4 only are correct<br>D 4 only is correct<br>E some other response |
|---|---|

**6** Consider the energy profile shown, which relates to the reaction:

$$2NO_2(g) \rightleftharpoons N_2O_4(g)$$

True statements about this reaction include:

(1) the forward reaction is endothermic

(2) the activation energy for the forward reaction is $a$

(3) adding a catalyst reduces both $a$ and $b$

(4) the activation energy of the reverse reaction is $a + b$

▨ A      ▨ B      ▨ C      ▨ D      ▨ E

What happens to the rate of a chemical reaction if the activation energy is lowered?

...................................................................................................................................................

...................................................................................................................................................

**7** True statements about catalysts include:

(1) the activation energy for a process is lowered by providing an alternative route

(2) the final mass of the catalyst is the same as the initial mass

(3) the catalyst will be chemically unchanged at the end of the reaction

(4) a specific catalyst often catalyses many different chemical reactions

▨ A      ▨ B      ▨ C      ▨ D      ▨ E

Name the catalyst used in the Haber process.

...................................................................................................................................................

...................................................................................................................................................

**8** The first step in the mechanism by which ozone, $O_3(g)$, reacts with chlorine radicals is:

$O_3 + Cl\bullet \longrightarrow ClO\bullet + O_2$

True statements about this process include:

(1) the chlorine radical has an unpaired electron

(2) $ClO\bullet$ may react with another ozone molecule

(3) it is a propagation step

(4) chlorine acts as a heterogeneous catalyst in the overall process

      A         B         C         D         E

What name is given to the stage in the mechanism in which two radicals combine?

..................................................................................................................

..................................................................................................................

**9** Consider the reaction:

$CaCO_3(s) + 2HCl(aq) \longrightarrow CaCl_2(aq) + H_2O(l) + CO_2(g)$

It could be followed by:

(1) using a mass balance to record the mass loss with time

(2) measuring the pH change with time

(3) using a gas syringe to record the volume of gas produced with time

(4) measuring the colour change with time

      A         B         C         D         E

Generally, what happens to the rate of reaction with time? Explain your answer.

..................................................................................................................

..................................................................................................................

..................................................................................................................

..................................................................................................................

**10** The rate of a chemical reaction may be considerably affected by an increase in temperature. Reasons for this include:

(1) particles gain kinetic energy

(2) particles collide more frequently per unit time

(3) the combined energy of collision is greater at the higher temperature

(4) more particles are involved in inelastic collisions at the higher temperature

      A         B         C         D         E

Why do not all colliding particles result in a reaction?

..................................................................................................................

..................................................................................................................

..................................................................................................................

..................................................................................................................

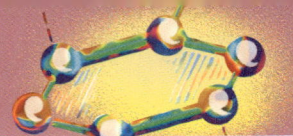

**11** The amount of dissolved carbon dioxide in $10\,cm^3$ of water changes from $2.00 \times 10^{-4}\,mol$ to $2.00 \times 10^{-5}\,mol$ in 100 seconds. Correct statements about this reaction include:
(1) the initial concentration of carbon dioxide solution was $2.00 \times 10^{-2}\,mol\,dm^{-3}$
(2) the change in the amount of carbon dioxide was $1.00 \times 10^{-5}\,mol$
(3) the final concentration of carbon dioxide solution was $2.00 \times 10^{-4}\,mol\,dm^{-3}$
(4) the average rate of reaction over the 100 seconds was $1.80 \times 10^{-4}\,mol\,dm^{-3}\,s^{-1}$

    A        B        C        D        E

If $2.00 \times 10^{-4}\,mol$ of carbon dioxide are dissolved in $10\,cm^3$ of water, what amount of carbon dioxide is required to make $150\,cm^3$ of solution of the same concentration?

**12** The most concentrated solution of glucose is:
    A 1 g of glucose in $50\,cm^3$ of water
    B 2 g of glucose in $50\,cm^3$ of water
    C 1 g of glucose in $25\,cm^3$ of water
    D 1 g of glucose in $12.5\,cm^3$ of water
    E 2 g of glucose in $100\,cm^3$ of water

Show your working.

**13** Powdered manganese(IV) oxide is added to a solution of hydrogen peroxide and a gas is formed. The reaction is then repeated using lumps of manganese(IV) oxide of the same total mass as the powder. Which of statements A–E is true about the latter compared with the former?
    A a greater volume of gas will form
    B the activation energy will be greater
    C the reaction will be faster
    D the reaction will be less exothermic (more positive)
    E the reaction will be slower

Write an equation to show the decomposition of hydrogen peroxide.

**14** When $25\,cm^3$ of sodium thio-sulphate solution is added to $25\,cm^3$ of dilute hydrochloric acid, a precipitate of sulphur forms. Which of A–E will reduce the rate at which the sulphur is formed?
    A $50\,cm^3$ of each solution is used instead of $25\,cm^3$
    B each solution is boiled to remove some water before mixing takes place
    C ice cubes are added to the mixture
    D the mixture is heated strongly
    E the reaction is continuously swirled

In an experiment, $0.01\,mol$ of sulphur forms in 4.0 seconds. What is the average rate of reaction expressed in $mol\,s^{-1}$?

**15** In a graph showing the volume of a gas changing with time, which of the following gives a value that is equal to the average rate ($cm^3 s^{-1}$) over the first 10 seconds?

- A the total volume of gas produced
- B the total volume produced multiplied by 10 seconds
- C the total volume of gas produced divided by 10 seconds
- D the time taken divided by the volume of gas
- E the number of moles of gas divided by 10 seconds

What is the difference between instantaneous rate and average rate of reaction?

..................................................................................................................................

..................................................................................................................................

..................................................................................................................................

..................................................................................................................................

**16** A reaction is carried out in which hydrogen peroxide solution decomposes in the presence of a manganese(IV) oxide catalyst. The fastest rate of reaction will be produced by:

- A 1 g of manganese(IV) oxide; 10 $cm^3$ of hydrogen peroxide solution; cool the mixture
- B 1 g of manganese(IV) oxide; 5 $cm^3$ of hydrogen peroxide and 5 $cm^3$ of water; cool the mixture
- C 2 g of manganese(IV) oxide; 10 $cm^3$ of hydrogen peroxide solution; warm the mixture
- D 2 g of manganese(IV) oxide; 5 $cm^3$ of hydrogen peroxide and 5 $cm^3$ of water; warm the mixture
- E 2 g of manganese(IV) oxide, 10 $cm^3$ of hydrogen peroxide solution and 5 $cm^3$ of water; warm the mixture

What is the significance of the (IV) in manganese(IV) oxide?

..................................................................................................................................

..................................................................................................................................

**17** The metal most likely to behave as a catalyst is:

- A calcium
- B potassium
- C aluminium
- D vanadium
- E lead

Name one of the catalysts used in a catalytic converter in a car.

..................................................................................................................................

..................................................................................................................................

**18** In a reaction involving an enzyme, as the temperature is increased, the rate of reaction increases and then drops dramatically. One reason for the rate decrease at a higher temperature is:

- A the enzyme expands, thereby increasing its surface area
- B the enzyme is killed
- C the enzyme is broken down into smaller fragments
- D the shape of the enzyme's active site changes
- E particles moving with a high kinetic energy collide with the active site

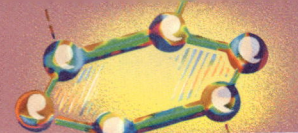

To which class of organic compounds do enzymes belong?

# Chemical equilibria and acids

Instructions for answering
questions 1–10:

A 1, 2 and 3 only are correct
B 1 and 3 only are correct
C 2 and 4 only are correct
D 4 only is correct
E some other response

Questions 1–5 concern the following reactions at equilibrium:
(1) $2NO_2(g) \rightleftharpoons N_2O_4(g)$  $\Delta H$ is negative
(2) $2O_3(g) \rightleftharpoons 3O_2(g)$  $\Delta H$ is negative
(3) $N_2(g) + 3H_2(g) \rightleftharpoons 2NH_3(g)$  $\Delta H$ is negative
(4) $H_2(g) + I_2(g) \rightleftharpoons 2HI(g)$  $\Delta H$ is positive

**1** Select the reaction(s) in which the equilibrium position moves to the right when the total pressure is increased.

☐ A        ☐ B        ☐ C        ☐ D        ☐ E

Briefly explain your answer.

**2** Select the reaction(s) in which the equilibrium position is not affected when the total pressure is decreased.

☐ A        ☐ B        ☐ C        ☐ D        ☐ E

Briefly explain your answer.

**3** Select the reaction(s) in which the forward and reverse rates of reaction decrease on reducing the temperature.

⬚ A          ⬚ B          ⬚ C          ⬚ D          ⬚ E

Briefly explain your answer.

.........................................................................................................................................................................

.........................................................................................................................................................................

.........................................................................................................................................................................

.........................................................................................................................................................................

**4** Select the reaction(s) in which the yield of product increases on decreasing the temperature.

⬚ A          ⬚ B          ⬚ C          ⬚ D          ⬚ E

Briefly explain your answer.

.........................................................................................................................................................................

.........................................................................................................................................................................

.........................................................................................................................................................................

.........................................................................................................................................................................

**5** Select the reaction(s) with a yield that varies according to the following graph:

⬚ A          ⬚ B          ⬚ C          ⬚ D          ⬚ E

Briefly explain your answer.

.........................................................................................................................................................................

.........................................................................................................................................................................

.........................................................................................................................................................................

.........................................................................................................................................................................

**6** The reaction $2HI(g) \rightleftharpoons H_2(g) + I_2(g)$ has an enthalpy change of $-52$ kJ per mole of hydrogen formed. Without any catalyst, the activation energy is 183 kJ mol$^{-1}$; with a gold catalyst, the activation energy is 105 kJ mol$^{-1}$. Given this information, correct statements include:
(1)  the activation energy of the reverse uncatalysed process is 235 kJ mol$^{-1}$
(2)  the forward and reverse reaction rates are affected equally when the temperature is increased
(3)  the enthalpy change will be $-52$ kJ in the presence of a gold catalyst
(4)  the gold catalyst moves the equilibrium position to the right-hand side

⬚ A          ⬚ B          ⬚ C          ⬚ D          ⬚ E

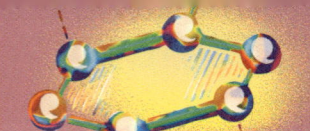

On a molecular scale, suggest how gold catalyses this reaction.

**7** Consider the reaction:

$$2N_2O(g) \rightleftharpoons 2N_2(g) + O_2(g) \quad \Delta H_f(N_2O) = +81.6 \, kJ \, mol^{-1}$$

Correct statements about this equilibrium include:
(1) the forward reaction is exothermic
(2) increasing the temperature increases the rate of the reverse reaction
(3) increasing the total pressure shifts the equilibrium position to the left
(4) adding a catalyst results in the enthalpy change being more positive

    A        B        C        D        E

What is the enthalpy change for the reaction as written?

**8** The table shows how the percentage yield of ammonia varies with both pressure and temperature in the process:

$$N_2(g) + 3H_2(g) \rightleftharpoons 2NH_3(g)$$

| Pressure/atm | Temperature/°C | | | | |
|---|---|---|---|---|---|
| | 300 | 400 | 500 | 600 | 700 |
| 1 | 2.18 | 0.44 | 0.13 | 0.05 | 0.02 |
| 10 | 14.7 | 3.85 | 1.21 | 0.49 | 0.23 |
| 1000 | 92.6 | 79.8 | 57.5 | 31.4 | 12.9 |

From these data, it can be deduced that:
(1) the forward process is exothermic
(2) increasing the pressure, at a fixed temperature, increases the yield of ammonia
(3) a maximum yield of ammonia is obtained using a maximum pressure and a minimum temperature
(4) the initial addition of a catalyst would have resulted in different yield figures being obtained

    A        B        C        D        E

Give a use for the ammonia formed in this process.

**9** Consider the equilibrium between the blue $[Cu(H_2O)_6]^{2+}$ ion and the yellow $[CuCl_4]^{2-}$ ion:

$$[Cu(H_2O)_6]^{2+}(aq) + 4Cl^-(aq) \rightleftharpoons [CuCl_4]^{2-}(aq) + 6H_2O(l) \quad \Delta H \text{ is positive}$$

When a particular equilibrium mixture is obtained, it is green in colour due to an equal concentration of both the yellow and blue ions. A yellow solution would be obtained when:

(1) the mixture is heated

(2) silver(I) nitrate solution is added

(3) the total pressure is increased

(4) a catalyst is added to the equilibrium mixture

A          B          C          D          E

What effect does increasing the temperature have on the activation energy of the forward process in this reaction?

..................................................................................................................................................

..................................................................................................................................................

**10**

The graphs show how the equilibrium percentage yield of a product, AB(g), formed from its constituent gaseous elements, $A_2(g)$ and $B_2(g)$, is affected by an increase in pressure and temperature. True statements include:

(1) the formation of AB is endothermic

(2) there are equal numbers of moles of A and B on each side of the balanced equation

(3) an increase in pressure increases both the forward and reverse rates of reaction

(4) the enthalpy of formation of AB is positive

A          B          C          D          E

Write an equation that represents the standard enthalpy of formation of AB(g).

..................................................................................................................................................

..................................................................................................................................................

**11** The products of the reaction between sodium carbonate and dilute sulphuric acid are:

    A $Na_2SO_4$; $H_2$; $CO_2$

    B $NaSO_4$; $CO_2$; $H_2O$

    C $Na_2SO_4$; $H_2O$; $CO_2$

    D $NaSO_4$; $H_2$; $H_2O$

    E $Na_2SO_4$; $O_2$; $H_2O$

Write an equation for this reaction.

..................................................................................................................................................

..................................................................................................................................................

**12** Typical conditions for the Haber process include:

    A 0°C and 35 atm

    B 450°C and 350 atm

    C 1000°C and 1000 atm

    D 450°C and 1 atm

    E 100°C and 100 atm

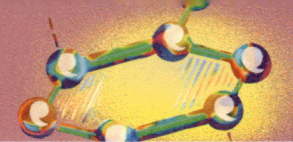

Why is a pressure of 1 000 000 atm not used in the Haber process?

................................................................................................................................

................................................................................................................................

**13** The ionic equation that
represents the reaction between
dilute hydrochloric acid and
copper(II) oxide is:

   A $CuO(s) + 2H^+(aq) \longrightarrow Cu^{2+}(aq) + H_2O(l)$
   B $OH^-(aq) + H^+(aq) \longrightarrow H_2O(l)$
   C $CuO(s) + 2H^+(aq) \longrightarrow Cu^{2+}(aq) + H_2O(l)$
   D $Cu^{2+}(aq) + 2H^+(aq) \longrightarrow Cu^{2+}(aq) + H_2(g)$
   E $Cu^{2+}(aq) + 2e^- \longrightarrow Cu(s)$

Is this a redox reaction? Explain your answer.

................................................................................................................................

................................................................................................................................

**14** 25 cm$^3$ of 0.10 mol dm$^{-3}$ sodium hydroxide solution is titrated with 0.10 mol dm$^{-3}$ ethanoic acid.
The equation for the reaction is:

   $CH_3COOH(aq) + NaOH(aq) \longrightarrow CH_3COONa(aq) + H_2O(l)$

The volume of ethanoic acid
solution required for complete
neutralisation is:

   A less than 15 cm$^3$
   B less than 25 cm$^3$ but more than 15 cm$^3$
   C exactly 25 cm$^3$
   D more than 25 cm$^3$ but less than 30 cm$^3$
   E more than 30 cm$^3$

Write an equation to show the dissociation of ethanoic acid in water.

................................................................................................................................

................................................................................................................................

**15** In an experiment, 25.0 cm$^3$ of 1.00 mol dm$^{-3}$ sulphuric
acid is added to 50.0 cm$^3$ of 1.00 mol dm$^{-3}$ sodium
hydroxide.
   $2NaOH(aq) + H_2SO_4(aq) \longrightarrow Na_2SO_4(aq) + 2H_2O(l)$
The likely pH of the resulting mixture is:

   A 1
   B 4
   C 7
   D 11
   E 14

Write the ionic equation for this reaction.

................................................................................................................................

................................................................................................................................

**16** Ammonia is a weak base that dissociates in water according to the equation:
   $NH_3(aq) + H_2O(l) \rightleftharpoons NH_4^+(aq) + OH^-(aq)$   $\Delta H$ is negative

The pH of the mixture is
lowered by:

   A warming the mixture
   B adding solid ammonium chloride, $NH_4Cl$
   C adding a catalyst
   D increasing the total pressure
   E adding ice to the mixture

What is the shape of the $H_3O^+$(aq) ion? Explain your answer.

...........................................................................................................................................

...........................................................................................................................................

**17** The correct formula of the salt aluminium sulphate is:

   A $AlSO_4$
   B $Al_2SO_4$
   C $Al(SO_4)_2$
   D $Al_2(SO_4)_3$
   E $Al(SO_4)_3$

What type of bonding occurs within the sulphate(VI) ion?

...........................................................................................................................................

...........................................................................................................................................

**18** Consider the reaction:
   $2NO_2(g) \rightleftharpoons N_2O_4(g)$
Which of A–E will result in no change in equilibrium position?

   A increasing the total pressure
   B adding a greater amount of nitrogen dioxide at constant volume
   C heating the mixture
   D adding a catalyst
   E removing the $N_2O_4$ as soon as it is formed

What is meant by the term 'equilibrium position'?

...........................................................................................................................................

...........................................................................................................................................

# General questions

**1** Carbon dioxide dissolves in water, giving the following equilibrium:
   $CO_2(aq) + H_2O(l) \rightleftharpoons HCO_3^-(aq) + H^+(aq)$   $\Delta H$ is negative
The equilibrium position can be moved to the right by:
(1) adding ice to the mixture
(2) adding a small amount of dilute sodium hydroxide solution
(3) adding more $CO_2$ to the solution
(4) boiling the mixture

   A        B        C        D        E

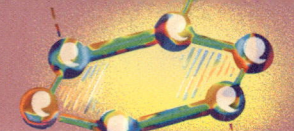

What effect, if any, does adding more water have on the enthalpy change for the reaction?

**2** Consider the equilibrium $2SO_2(g) + O_2(g) \rightleftharpoons 2SO_3(g)$ $\Delta H = -196\,kJ$
(r.a.m. S = 32, O = 16)
True statements about this equilibrium include:
(1) increasing the temperature results in more $SO_3$ forming
(2) $\Delta H$ for the reverse reaction is also −196 kJ
(3) if 64 g of oxygen were used, $2 \times (-196)\,kJ$ of heat would be released
(4) when 128 g of $SO_2$ is added to 32 g of $O_2$, 160 g of $SO_3$ should form at equilibrium

⬛ A          ⬛ B          ⬛ C          ⬛ D          ⬛ E

Name the industrial process of sulphuric(VI) acid manufacture that uses this reaction.

**3** The pH of a $1.0\,mol\,dm^{-3}$ solution of hydrochloric acid is approximately 1; the pH of a $1\,mol\,dm^{-3}$ solution of ethanoic acid is approximately 3. Reasons for the difference in pH include:
(1) the dissociation of ethanoic acid is reversible
(2) the chloride ion is a weaker conjugate base than the ethanoate ion
(3) ethanoic acid is a weaker acid than hydrochloric acid
(4) ethanoic acid produces a solution of lower pH

⬛ A          ⬛ B          ⬛ C          ⬛ D          ⬛ E

Define a Brønsted–Lowry base.

**4** The enthalpy of neutralisation for any strong acid reacting with any strong alkali is always approximately −57 kJ mol$^{-1}$. Explanations for this include:
(1) the same bonds are being formed in each reaction
(2) the enthalpy of formation of all products and reactants in each reaction will be the same
(3) the ionic equation for each reaction is $H^+(aq) + OH^-(aq) \longrightarrow H_2O(l)$
(4) each reaction takes place at a similar rate

⬛ A          ⬛ B          ⬛ C          ⬛ D          ⬛ E

Suggest an approximate value for the enthalpy change for the reaction:
$CH_3COOH(aq) + NH_3(aq) \longrightarrow CH_3COO^-NH_4^+(aq)$

**5** True statements about the process $Cl_2(g) \rightleftharpoons 2Cl(g)$ include:

(1) the process is expected to be endothermic

(2) an increase in total pressure should affect the equilibrium position

(3) increasing the temperature should affect the equilibrium position

(4) increasing the total pressure will have no effect on either the forward or reverse process

▨ A        ▨ B        ▨ C        ▨ D        ▨ E

Name this type of process.

......................................................................................................................................................

......................................................................................................................................................

**6** Two allotropes of sulphur (rhombic and monoclinic) are in equilibrium with each other at a particular temperature (95.6°C), which is called the transition temperature.

$S_{rhombic} \rightleftharpoons S_{monoclinic}$

$(\Delta H_f [S_{rhombic}] = 0 \, kJ \, mol^{-1}; \Delta H_f [S_{monoclinic}] = +0.3 \, kJ \, mol^{-1})$

True statements about this equilibrium include:

(1) at the transition temperature, the forward and reverse reactions occur at different rates

(2) the conversion of $S_{rhombic}$ to $S_{monoclinic}$ is endothermic

(3) increasing the temperature causes more rhombic sulphur to form

(4) increasing the temperature increases the rate of both the forward and reverse processes

▨ A        ▨ B        ▨ C        ▨ D        ▨ E

Which allotrope of sulphur should evolve more heat energy when equivalent masses are completely combusted in excess oxygen?

......................................................................................................................................................

......................................................................................................................................................

**7**

| Temperature/°C | Mass of nitrogen per 1 g water |
|:---:|:---:|
| 0 | $2.95 \times 10^{-5}$ |
| 40 | $1.39 \times 10^{-5}$ |
| 70 | $8.5 \times 10^{-6}$ |
| 90 | $3.8 \times 10^{-6}$ |

The table shows how the solubility of nitrogen gas varies with temperature. The equilibrium operating is $N_2(g) \rightleftharpoons N_2(aq)$.

True statements about this equilibrium include:

(1) the rate at which equilibrium is attained increases as the total pressure is increased

(2) a decrease in temperature results in an increase in the rate at which equilibrium is achieved

(3) the forward reaction is exothermic

(4) the solubility of nitrogen at 90°C is approximately twice that at 40°C

▨ A        ▨ B        ▨ C        ▨ D        ▨ E

What mass of nitrogen is required to completely saturate $100 \, cm^3$ of water at 40°C?

........................................................................................................................................................

........................................................................................................................................................

Questions 8 –12 are concerned with the following graphs:

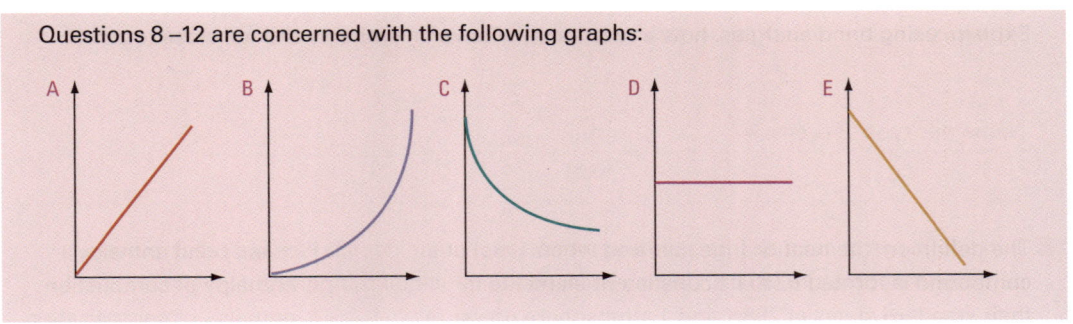

**8** Select the graph that shows how the amount of $NO_2(g)$ varies with pressure in the reaction:
$NO_2(g) + 2CO(g) \rightleftharpoons \frac{1}{2}N_2(g) + 2CO_2(g)$

                A           B           C           D           E

What is the SI unit for amount of substance?

........................................................................................................................................................

........................................................................................................................................................

**9** Select the graph that shows how the concentration of a reactant, decaying according to first-order kinetics, varies with time (i.e. obeying the rate equation: rate = $k$[reactant]).

                A           B           C           D           E

In this particular case, is the rate directly proportional to the concentration of reactant?

........................................................................................................................................................

........................................................................................................................................................

**10** Select the graph that shows, for a typical reaction, the rate of reaction against temperature.

                A           B           C           D           E

What factor determines the sensitivity of reaction rate to increasing temperature?

........................................................................................................................................................

........................................................................................................................................................

**11** Select the graph that shows the rate against (concentration)$^2$, given the rate equation:
rate = $k$[reactant]$^2$

                A           B           C           D           E

Given this particular graph, how would the rate constant, $k$, be determined?

........................................................................................................................................................

........................................................................................................................................................

**12** Select the graph that shows the equilibrium amount of reactant against temperature for a reaction that has an enthalpy change close to zero.

A          B          C          D          E

Explain, using bond energies, how a reaction may have an enthalpy change close to zero.

..............................................................................................................................

..............................................................................................................................

..............................................................................................................................

..............................................................................................................................

**13** The definition 'the heat change involved when 1 mol of a compound is formed from its constituent elements in their standard states at 298 K and 1 atmosphere pressure' describes:

A mean bond enthalpy
B enthalpy of combustion
C enthalpy of neutralisation
D enthalpy of reaction
E enthalpy of formation

Suggest whether or not a standard enthalpy change is dependent on the conditions of temperature and pressure at which it is measured.

..............................................................................................................................

..............................................................................................................................

**14** The reaction

$H_2(g) + S(s) \longrightarrow H_2S(g)$

has a standard enthalpy change of $-20.2\,kJ\,mol^{-1}$. A correct statement about this reaction is:

A the reaction is likely to be very fast
B $H_2S(g)$ has a positive enthalpy of formation
C $H_2S(g)$ has a higher chemical energy than its constituent elements
D no bonds are either broken or made in this reaction
E the rate of reaction may be very slow at room temperature

What factor determines the rate at which a reaction proceeds?

..............................................................................................................................

..............................................................................................................................

**15** A false statement about the nature of a chemical bond is:

A bond making is always exothermic
B highly exothermic reactions involve stronger bonds being made in the products than existing bonds in the reactants
C only heat can break a chemical bond
D all bonds exist as a result of electrostatic attractions
E bond breaking is always endothermic

Give the names of the two main types of chemical bond.

..............................................................................................................................

..............................................................................................................................

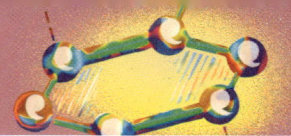

Questions 16–18 are concerned with the following energy cycle:

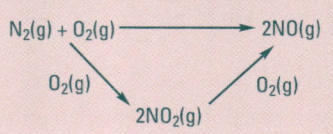

The standard enthalpies of formation of NO(g) and $NO_2(g)$ are +90.4 kJ $mol^{-1}$ and +33.9 kJ $mol^{-1}$ respectively.

**16** $N_2(g) + O_2(g) \longrightarrow 2NO(g)$
The standard enthalpy change (in kJ $mol^{-1}$) for this reaction is:

A  −90.4
B  +90.4
C  −45.2
D  +180.8
E  +45.2

Show your working.

...........................................................................................................

...........................................................................................................

**17** $2NO(g) + O_2(g) \longrightarrow 2NO_2(g)$
The enthalpy change (in kJ $mol^{-1}$) for this reaction is given by:

A  90.4 − 33.9
B  $(2 \times 33.9) - (2 \times 90.4)$
C  90.4 + 33.9
D  $(2 \times 90.4) - (2 \times 33.9)$
E  33.9 − 90.4

What will be the enthalpy change for the reaction: $NO_2(g) \longrightarrow NO(g) + \frac{1}{2}O_2(g)$

...........................................................................................................

...........................................................................................................

**18** $H_2O(g) + 2NO(g) + \frac{3}{2}O_2(g) \longrightarrow 2HNO_3(l)$
The standard enthalpy change for this reaction is −284.8 kJ. Given that the enthalpy of formation for gaseous water is −242 kJ $mol^{-1}$, the standard enthalpy of formation of nitric acid, $HNO_3$, is:

A  −436.4
B  −73.4
C  −173
D  +218.2
E  −346

Show your working.

...........................................................................................................

...........................................................................................................

Philip Allan Updates
Market Place, Deddington, Oxfordshire, OX15 0SE

*Orders*
Bookpoint Ltd
130 Milton Park, Abingdon, Oxfordshire, OX14 4SB
tel: 01235 827720   fax: 01235 400454
e-mail: uk.orders@bookpoint.co.uk
Lines are open 9.00 a.m.–5.00 p.m., Monday to Saturday, with a 24-hour message answering service. You can also order through the Philip Allan Updates website:
www.philipallan.co.uk

© Philip Allan Updates 2004   ISBN 978-1-84489-110-8

Printed in Spain